CULTURES OF THE WORLD®

RWANDA

David C. King

Marshall Cavendish
Benchmark
New York

PICTURE CREDITS

Cover photo: © David Keith Jones / Alamy

AFP: 26, 31, 41, 115, 117, 122, 129 • age fotostock: 10 • alt.TYPE / Reuters: 30, 33, 37, 42, 44, 89, 118 • Bes Stock: 113, 130 • Corbis Inc.: 1, 25, 27, 28, 34, 43, 47, 50, 74, 78, 81, 88, 98, 100, 119, 126 • Eye Ubiquitous / Hutchison Library: 79 • Getty Images: 19, 21, 22, 23, 24, 29, 39, 46, 52, 60, 66, 76, 95 • Hutchison Library: 6, 8, 12, 32, 36, 40, 48, 49, 51, 53, 58, 62, 63, 65, 68, 69, 70, 72, 86, 90, 104, 106, 108, 110, 112 • IMAGES24.co.za / Eric Miller: 92 • Evert Jakobs – www.rwanda-gorillas.com: 59 • Giacomo Pirozzi / Panos Pictures: 54 • Julie Pulowski / UNDP Rwanda: 45 • J-F. Rollinger / ANA Photo Agency: 17, 82, 93, 99 • The Rotary Club of Kigali-Virunga: 102 • Lonely Planet Images: 3, 4, 5, 13, 18, 64, 80, 83, 84, 91, 97, 120, 124, 127 • Minden Pictures: 11, 14, 15, 16, 67 • National Geographic Images: 56 • North Wind Picture Archives: 20 • Andrade, Gustavo / Stockfood: 131 • www.tropix.co.uk / D. Charlwood: 128

PRECEDING PAGE

Jubilant Rwandan schoolchildren pose for the camera.

Marshall Cavendish Benchmark
99 White Plains Road
Tarrytown, NY 10591
Website: www.marshallcavendish.us

© Marshall Cavendish International (Asia) Private Limited 2006
® "Cultures of the World" is a registered trademark of Marshall Cavendish Corporation.

Series concept and design by Times Editions
An imprint of Marshall Cavendish International (Asia) Private Limited
A member of Times Publishing Limited

All Internet sites were correct and accurate at the time of printing.

Library of Congress Cataloging-in-Publication Data
King, David C.
   Rwanda / By David C. King
      p. cm. — (Cultures of the world)
   Summary: "Provides comprehensive information on the geography, history, governmental
      structure, economy, cultural diversity, peoples, religion, and culture of Rwanda"—Provided
      by publisher.
   Includes bibliographical references and index.
   ISBN-13: 978-0-7614-2333-1
   ISBN-10: 0-7614-2333-8
   1. Rwanda—Juvenile literature. I. Title. II. Series.
   DT450.14.K56 2007
   967.571—dc22   2005031817

Printed in China

7 6 5 4 3 2 1

CONTENTS

A woman and her child in Kigali. Familial bonds are strong in Rwandan society.

3

A river runs through Nyungwe Forest. Rwanda's relatively pristine nature reserves and unique wildlife are major draws for tourists.

INTRODUCTION

FOR MANY PEOPLE the name Rwanda is associated with a terrifying episode of mass murder that took place in the mid-1990s. While the world looked the other way, this small, landlocked African nation was the scene of a civil war and genocide that claimed more than 800,000 lives—nearly one out of every 10 Rwandans was slaughtered.

Over the past decade the people of Rwanda have made enormous progress in rebuilding their devastated nation. They are determined to make Rwanda a model of healing. The heroism of the people, combined with the richness of the culture and the natural beauty of the land, give them plenty of material to work with.

GEOGRAPHY

RWANDA IS A LAND of natural wonders. It has a landscape of beautiful, rolling hills and a climate that is surprisingly cool and comfortable for a country located so close to the equator. Dense mountain rain forest and savanna grasslands are home to more than 80 species of mammals, including elephants, lions, giraffes, hippopotamuses, and crocodiles, as well as hundreds of bird species. The picturesque scenery includes sparkling lakes and rivers, volcanic mountains, coffee and tea plantations, lively outdoor markets, plus colorful dancers and music. And nearly hidden in the mists of the mountains are the magnificent mountain gorillas.

This small, landlocked nation, slightly smaller than the state of Maryland, is located in the very heart of Africa; it is 1,250 miles (2,000 km) east of the Atlantic Ocean and 880 miles (1,415 km) west of the Indian Ocean. With a population of more than 8 million people, it has a population density of 826 people per square mile (319 per square km). That makes Rwanda one of the two most densely populated countries on the African continent.

On the west Rwanda is bounded by the Democratic Republic of the Congo, on the north by Uganda, on the east by Tanzania, and on the south by Burundi.

RWANDA AND THE GREAT RIFT VALLEY

On a physical map of Africa you can see a ridge that separates the Nile River basin, or watershed, from the basin of the Congo River. This ridge, which is part of the Great Rift Valley, cuts from north to south through western Rwanda at an average altitude of 9,000 feet (2,743 m) above sea level. On the western edge of this ridge, the land slopes sharply to Lake Kivu and the Ruzizi Valley. The eastern edge slopes more gradually, with rolling hills extending like waves across central plateaus, a landscape that has led Rwanda to be called "the Land of a Thousand Hills."

Opposite: **Rwanda's rolling landscape results in a cool, mild climate.**

Lake Kivu, one of the Great Lakes of Africa, is located at the Great Rift Valley.

The entire landscape of rivers, high plateaus, and mountains is a product of Rwanda's position in the Great Rift Valley, which slices through Africa, from the Red Sea in the north to Mozambique in the south. A ring of volcanic mountains, known as the Virunga Range, was created by the same geologic pressure that produced the Great Rift Valley more than 20 million years ago.

GEOGRAPHIC REGIONS

Lake Kivu, the country's largest lake, and the Ruzizi River form Rwanda's western border with Democratic Republic of the Congo. From this boundary on the edge of the Great Rift Valley, the land rises sharply to about 9,000 feet (2,700 m). The lake, with its jagged shoreline, has great mountain views and excellent sand beaches.

South of the lake region lies Nyungwe Forest, a large area of mountain rain forest sprawled across mountains that stretch south to the border with Burundi. The forest is famous for its variety of plants and animals, including the black-and-white Angolan colobus monkey, which forms

THE GREAT RIFT VALLEY

The huge fault line that created the geographic feature known as the Great Rift Valley was formed when two of the earth's tectonic plates separated. As the plates pulled apart, large pieces of the earth's crust slid down between the plates. This resulted in the formation of escarpments (steep slopes or long cliffs) and ravines, often with dramatically sheer sides. The western part of the Rift Valley, known as the Albertine Rift Valley, extends from Lake Albert in Uganda, through Rwanda, south to Lake Tanganyika, and beyond to Lake Malawi.

Earthquakes and volcanic eruptions are not uncommon today, a sign that the plates are moving. If they keep moving apart, East Africa could separate from the rest of the continent in several million years.

huge troops of up to 400. This is one of the oldest forest regions in Africa, making it a favorite area for scientific research.

North of Lake Kivu is the Virunga Range, a chain of seven volcanic mountains created by the same forces that produced the Great Rift Valley. The mountains rise to an elevation of 14,800 feet (4,510 m).

The center of Rwanda is a series of plateaus that range in elevation from 5,000 to 7,000 feet (1,500 to 2,100 m) above sea level. This plateau region was once covered by forest, but most of the land has been cleared for farming, especially over the past century. Each plateau slopes from west to east and ends in an escarpment with marshland at the base. The capital, Kigali, is located in this plateau region.

Several small lakes in the central region have irregular borders created by the very steep hills surrounding them. Because of the pressing need for cropland, the slopes have been carefully terraced. Terrace crops include plantains, beans, and sweet potatoes. Most of this region is savanna grassland, with a few dense woods and scattered acacia thorn trees.

Only in the east do the hills and mountains give way to lower, flatter land. This is part of a huge lowland area called the Lake Victoria Basin. The Akagera River, with its many large papyrus swamps and small lakes, forms Rwanda's border with Tanzania. Much of the region is protected in the Akagera National Park. The park is home to a great variety of plant and animal species.

A misty tea plantation in Rwanda. Unlike most countries situated near the equator, Rwanda's climate is temperate rather than tropical.

CLIMATE

Altitude is an important influence on climate, and Rwanda's highlands and mountains have a remarkably comfortable climate, despite being within a few degrees of the equator. In the Great Rift Valley in the west the average annual temperature is 73°F (23°C), and the average annual rainfall is about 30 inches (76 cm). In the mountains the temperature decreases with altitude to an average of about 63°F (17°C), and rainfall increases to an average of 58 inches (147 cm). On the central plateaus the temperature and rainfall averages are between those extremes.

In terms of climate Rwanda has four seasons: two wet and two dry. There is a short rainy season from October to December, followed by a short dry season in January and February. The long rainy season extends from March to May, and the long dry season lasts from June to September.

FLORA

The enormous variety of plant and animal species is divided into several unique ecosystems: Nyungwe Forest and the volcanic mountains of the west, the central highland grassland, and the lowlands of the east. The Nyungwe Forest National Park, for example, has at least 200 species of trees. The upper canopy of trees, reaching 200 feet (60 m), is dominated by slow-growing hardwoods such as African mahogany and Mulanje cedar. There is greater variety in the midstory canopy, and in the lower canopy there are giant tree ferns and large lobelias. The forest also has over 200 species of orchids and begonias.

The savanna grasslands of central and parts of eastern Rwanda have scattered acacia thorn trees and euphorbia, which are cactuslike plants that have a milky sap and flowers without petals. Much of this central area is now used for growing crops and for pasture. Above about 6,500 feet (2,000 m), bamboo is dominant.

The eastern region of Rwanda, warmer and wetter than the rest of the country, contains sprawling papyrus swamps that connect a series of small lakes. There are large areas of broad-leafed trees and smaller stands of acacia. Because it is isolated by mountains, several species of flowers, shrubs, and trees are endemic to (found only in) Akagera National Park.

The lush greenery of Volcanoes National Park.

FAUNA

The various animal species living in Rwanda are found largely in the forest and savanna regions. There are a total of 86 mammal species in the country. The populations of large animals, including elephants, lions, water buffalos, and giraffes have fallen dramatically in the past 30 or 40 years. Protected areas, such as Akagera National Park, have lost up to two-thirds of their land. Poachers and warfare have also taken their toll.

Even with these setbacks the variety of animal life is impressive. Akagera, for example, has 11 species of antelope, ranging from the eland, the world's largest antelope, to the tiny common duiker. This park, along with the adjacent Mutura Hunting Reserve, has a number of very rare species, such as the giant pangolin, a variety of anteater. The lakes support one of the largest populations of hippopotamus found anywhere

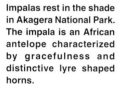

Impalas rest in the shade in Akagera National Park. The impala is an African antelope characterized by gracefulness and distinctive lyre shaped horns.

A l'Hoest's monkey in Nyungwe Forest National Park.

in Africa, as well as large crocodiles. The grasslands in the east still have small numbers of leopards, lions, and black rhinoceroses.

The forests and mountains of western Rwanda are most famous for their various primates. Nyungwe Forest National Park is home to 13 species, including the common chimpanzee and eight varieties of monkey. The colobus monkey, which lives in troops of 200 to 400, is known for its acrobatics in the forest canopy. It is easily recognized by its black coloring and white whiskers, shoulders, and tip of tail. Other monkey species include l'Hoest's monkey, a large primate with a gray and red coat contrasting with a white beard; the silver monkey; the rare owl-faced monkey; and the olive baboon.

The chimpanzees of Nyungwe are one of the most popular tourist attractions in all of Rwanda. Visitors can take guided or unguided "chimpanzee walks" through the park, observing troops ranging between 10 and 120 animals. The chimpanzees are more closely related to humans than to any other living creatures. They are known to use simple tools and, in captivity, have been taught to communicate with sign language.

A tree hyrax perches on a moss-covered tree branch. A native of Rwanda's forests, the tree hyrax is nocturnal.

The great study of chimpanzees, begun by Jane Goodall in 1960, continues today. While the research is centered in neighboring Tanzania, Rwanda has also been included in the study.

Nyungwe also has a variety of predators. Small numbers of leopards are still found in the forest, along with golden cats, wildcats, side-striped jackals, and three species of mongoose. Other mammals include the Congo clawless otter, giant forest hog, bushpig, and several types of squirrel. (The giant forest squirrel can glide from tree to tree, and the tree hyrax is a creature that looks like a guinea pig and has a bloodcurdling screech heard in many rain forest movies.)

Of all the animals in Rwanda, by far the most famous is the mountain gorilla. These largest of all primates once lived in a wide swath of land in central Africa, but there are now only about 700 of the peaceful creatures left. A little more than half of them live in Rwanda's Volcanoes National

Park, with slightly smaller numbers living in Uganda and the Democratic Republic of the Congo. In spite of the recent violence in Rwanda, mountain gorillas are again a major tourist attraction. Veterans of "gorilla treks" say that there are few experiences more magical than an encounter with a mountain gorilla.

One of the most remarkable features of Rwanda's wildlife is its variety of birds, with 670 species recorded. The birds in western Rwanda are different from those in the eastern lowlands. The Nyungwe Forest is home to 280 species, including 26 that are found only in this area of the Great Rift Valley. Some of the forest dwellers are known for their unusual colors, such as the great blue turaco, a large bird with bright blue, green, and yellow feathers. And a few species are found only in this forest and the volcanic mountains, including the Kivu ground thrush, the red-faced woodland warbler, and the yellow-eyed black flycatcher.

The colorful Montane sunbird is one of the many beautiful bird species that can be found in Rwanda's forests.

The birdlife of eastern Rwanda is quite different from that of the west. Many species are savanna dwellers, like the lilac-breasted roller and the black-headed gonalek, as are a number of raptors, including hooded vultures and brown snake eagles. Far more numerous are the water birds of the lakes and swamps. These include varieties of stork, crane, heron, egret, and shoebill.

Rwanda is also home to a wide variety of smaller creatures. There are well over 100 species of butterflies, as well as several kinds of large beetles and many varieties of ants, including the notorious army ant that marches through the forests in huge columns.

THE MOUNTAIN GORILLA

The magnificent mountain gorilla was unknown to the outside world until 1902, when a German explorer shot two. Over the next 50 years studies showed that mountain gorillas were a species separate from the slightly smaller lowland gorillas. Efforts to protect them began in the 1920s with the formation of Albert National Park (now Virunga National Park).

In 1959 George Schaller started the first scientific study of how mountain gorillas live. Dian Fossey continued his work, establishing a research center in 1967. For nearly twenty years she spent long periods in Volcanoes National Park, and her work made the world aware of the gorillas' nonaggressive behavior and their sedentary, highly social life. Her efforts were a key reason that poaching was sharply curtailed. (The mountain gorilla population had dropped dramatically in the 1950s and 1960s.)

Fossey was murdered in 1985, probably by the poachers she had struggled against for years. Three years later her efforts received worldwide publicity with release of the film *Gorillas in the Mist*. The film helped to create great interest in protecting mountain gorillas and in gorilla tourism. Guided treks to view these peaceful giants in their natural habitat have been Rwanda's major source of tourism revenue ever since, except for the mid-1990s, when the genocide forced the closing of the park.

CITIES

From the air Rwanda looks like a huge expanse of green, with many small trees indicating tea, coffee, and banana plantations. This is a rural country in which 9 out of every 10 families live by farming.

There are almost no large cities and, in the countryside, there are few compact towns or villages. Instead, houses are loosely clustered in family compounds, usually centered on a small hill. Each dwelling is encircled by an enclosure formed by a hedge, or palisade, of living plants. More enclosures extend to the rear of the dwelling owned by the head of the family. Livestock are also kept inside each family's enclosure.

Kigali was a town of about 25,000 when it was chosen as the capital of the newly independent nation in 1962. Its population has mushroomed to 656,000 people since then, but it still has much of the atmosphere of a small town and sprawls over several hills in the center of the country.

A busy commercial district in the capital of Rwanda, Kigali.

HISTORY

EAST AFRICA, including the portion of the Great Rift Valley that cuts through it, is often called the cradle of humanity. The fossils of ancient hominids, the early ancestors of modern humans, found there are more than 2.5 million years old. Scientists believe that groups of modern humans spread out to Asia and then to Europe beginning around 100,000 years ago.

Evidence of the earliest settlements in present-day Rwanda date to about 10,000 B.C. These ancient Rwandans were small in stature and lived by hunting and gathering. Descendants of these people, called the Twa, continue to make up a small percentage of Rwanda's population today. Around 700 B.C., Bantu-speaking farmers, the Hutu, discovered the region's fertile highlands, moved in, and pushed the Twa off the best farmland.

A few hundred years later another wave of migration brought pastoralists, or livestock raisers, into present-day Rwanda. These people, the Tutsi, soon gained dominance over the Hutu farmers. In the 15th century Ruganzu Bwimba, a Tutsi leader, established a kingdom near Kigali. Each king, or *mwami*, after him tried to expand the kingdom. By the 19th century Kigeri Rwabugiri, considered the country's greatest *mwami*, had expanded the kingdom almost to Rwanda's present borders.

Each king was the supreme authority and, in a magical way, was thought to embody Rwanda itself. All kings from about A.D. 1000 on appear to have been Tutsi. The king's authority was balanced, however, by a powerful queen and by a group called the *abiiru*, who had the task

Above: **Kigeri IV (center), the last king of Rwanda.**

Opposite: **A woman sits outside a re-construction of the palace of the *mwami* in Butare. The *mwamis* were the absolute rulers of Rwanda before the colonial period.**

19

of making sure that royal decrees did not violate the kingdom's code of laws or morals. The *abiiru* could reverse an order of the king and also controlled the selection of a new king. This unusual system of checks and balances seemed to work well, and so did a form of federalism that allowed local chiefs, or kings, to govern small areas.

Throughout the history of Rwanda's kingdoms the country remained closed to the outside world. There was very little trade with other kingdoms, and there was no monetary system. Outsiders who tried to enter, such as the American explorer Henry Stanley in 1874, were greeted by a storm of arrows. Rwanda maintained that isolation until the arrival of Europeans in the 1890s. It was also one of the few African countries that never sold its people, or its enemies, into slavery.

RWANDA FEUDALISM

The deep division between Hutu and Tutsi may have originated in Rwanda's unique version of feudalism, called *ubuhake*. This was a complex system that, in simplest terms, allowed an inferior to receive protection from a superior in exchange for services. This was not unlike feudalism in medieval Europe, in which peasants worked the land owned by nobles who kept the revenue in exchange for providing military service.

In Rwanda up to 1900 the Tutsi cattle raisers *(above)* were generally similar to the European nobles in the social and political structure. Europeans thought this class structure was based partly on physical differences: the Tutsi chiefs and nobles were very tall, especially in relation to the short, stocky Hutu farmers and the very much smaller Twa. The Hutu did control small areas in the north until 1911–12, when German troops helped the Tutsi overwhelm the region and incorporate it into Rwanda. The Hutu fought vigorously to hold on to their independence, and the bitterness between the cultural groups continued through the next half century.

Heinrich Albert Schnee, was governor of German East Africa, from 1912 to 1918.

THE GERMAN ERA

Throughout the second half of the 19th century the colonizing powers of Europe engaged in a race to carve up Africa into colonies to be exploited for their resources. Germany, which did not become a unified nation until the 1870s, was a late entry in the race but quickly insisted on some share of colonies. At a meeting called the Berlin Conference held in 1885, Germany was allowed to claim Ruanda-Urundi (as Rwanda and Burundi were then called) as part of German East Africa, even though no European officials had ever set foot there.

The era of German rule was brief and ended during World War I (1914–18). The Germans ruled through the existing power structure and had little impact on the country, except for allowing religious missions to set up bases. The missions, both Catholic and Protestant, established schools, medical centers, and farms.

BELGIAN RULE

While Germany was struggling for its survival during World War I, Belgium took control of Rwanda, partly in retaliation for Germany's invasion of neutral Belgium in 1914. In 1923 the League of Nations created Ruanda-Urundi as a League Mandate to be ruled by Belgium. The Belgians remained in control for 40 years; after World War II (1939–45) the League Mandate was replaced by a United Nations trusteeship in 1946.

Under Belgian rule Rwanda kept a separate budget and administration, although in 1925, it was linked to the Belgian Congo. Within what was still called Ruanda-Urundi, each native kingdom remained pretty much independent, with its own sovereign and systems of justice, taxation, and administration.

Belgian rule was beneficial to Rwanda in material ways. Agricultural production was increased, and a good deal of money and effort went into the building of roads, schools, hospitals, and government buildings. But in terms of human relationships, the Belgians managed to harden the lines between the Hutu and Tutsi. The colonial rulers wanted to make Rwanda more democratic, for example, so they encouraged Hutu leaders to participate in politics. By 1950 the Hutu, who formed a majority of

A school set up by Ursuline nuns in the Belgian Congo. Under colonial rule, Catholic missionary schools proliferated throughout the Congo and Ruanda-Urundi.

the population, were demanding a greater voice in government and an end to Tutsi political domination. Throughout the 1950s, the Belgians gradually switched their support from the still-powerful Tutsi minority to the Hutu majority.

INDEPENDENCE

The winds of change were sweeping across Africa in the 1950s and 1960s. One colony after another demanded independence from Europe's colonial powers. In Rwanda the movement for independence was complicated by the growing tensions between the Hutu majority, determined to

Belgians evacuate the Congo in 1960. The departure of the Belgians led to the formation of three sovereign nations: the Republic of Congo, the Republic of Burundi, and the Republic of Rwanda.

gain control of the country, and the Tutsi minority, which felt its power slipping away.

The first violence erupted late in 1959, when a Hutu subchief was beaten by a gang of Tutsi. Hutu gangs retaliated and rampaged through the country. Several hundred people were killed before Belgian authorities restored order. Like the Tutsi, the Belgians felt their power slipping away, and they turned to the UN for help. The UN refused to accept elections organized by the Hutu political party in 1960. New elections were held in 1961, but it was not until July 1962 that Rwanda's independence was recognized, the monarchy was abolished, and a republic was formed, with Grégoire Kayibanda as president.

In spite of UN involvement and the creation of an independent nation, troubles between the two ethnic groups continued. More than 100,000 Tutsi fled the Hutu assaults and sought refuge in neighboring countries. The new government, controlled by the Hutu, set strict employment quotas to address the long-standing inequalities with the Tutsi, who were allowed only 9 percent of jobs, school positions, and government appointments, reflecting the fact that they made up only 9 percent of the population. Other steps were taken to reinforce Hutu supremacy. Kayibanda was reelected president in 1965 and again in 1969, but his administration became increasingly brutal and corrupt, causing even the Hutu to demand moderation.

In 1973, after the government drove practically all the Tutsi out of education establishments, Major General Juvénal Habyarimana led a military coup that drove Kayibanda from power. A period of relative calm followed. Since the Hutu now had a virtual monopoly on power, Habyarimana was easily reelected as president in 1978, 1983, and 1988. It soon became clear that Habyarimana's regime was not much kinder to the Tutsi than was the previous one. In addition, the steady decline

The late French president François Mitterrand speaks with Juvénal Habyarimana *(second from the right)* **in Kigali on December 10, 1982. Habyarimana became president of Rwanda after staging a military coup against Grégoire Kayibanda in 1973.**

in prices for Rwanda's products, especially tea and coffee, brought the economy close to collapse.

On October 1, 1990 a group of Tutsi exiles, organized as the Rwandan Patriotic Front (RPF) and including some Hutu, launched an invasion from Uganda. The government received help from French, German, and Zairean (now called Congolese) troops, and the uprising was quickly suppressed. Thousands were imprisoned. Habyarimana promised reforms, but nothing happened. Instead, he strengthened the army and the army-trained militia called Interahamwe ("those who fought together") and secured additional support from French troops.

The RPF, now headed by Major Paul Kagame, continued its raids and its training of new recruits. Kagame insisted that the goal was to restore democracy rather than to bring back the Tutsi into power.

The co-founder of the RPF, Paul Kagame *(in dark olive colored uniform)* with his soldiers. Together with his friend Fred Rwigyema, Kagame established the RPF to unseat the Hutu-led government.

As the violence continued, pressure from Western countries and the UN led to an agreement made at Arusha, Tanzania, in August 1993. The Arusha Agreement committed Habyarimana to reforms, including integration of the army with RPF troops. A transitional national assembly was to begin the reforms, supported by a UN force. The hope created by the agreement quickly vanished when extremists refused to accept it. By late 1993 the atmosphere in Rwanda was one of impending doom.

RPF soldiers make preparations to engage government troops.

THE GENOCIDE

In the spring of 1994 many Tutsi Rwandans, including families of mixed Hutu-Tutsi marriages, began to flee the country. Government-controlled television and radio broadcast inflammatory messages denouncing the Tutsi as "the enemy." In a desperate bid for help Habyarimana went to a conference of regional presidents. On his return to Kigali, his jet plane was shot down by a surface-to-air missile on April 6. Both the Rwandan president and Cyprien Ntaryamira, the newly elected president of neighboring Burundi, died in the crash. Hours later the killing began. It was never determined who fired the deadly missile.

The well-planned violence against the Tutsi and any Hutu associated with them was led by the army commander Colonel Theoneste Bagosora. The goal was genocide—the killing of all the Tutsi. This was one of the few times in history that an attempt was made to destroy an entire ethnic group. One of Bagosora's first acts was to order the killing of Prime Minister Agathe Uwilingiyimana, a Hutu "moderate," followed by the

RPF soldiers scour the site of the plane crash that ended the lives of the presidents of Rwanda and Burundi.

29

A man tends to a memorial in Kigali dedicated to the ten Belgian UN peacekeepers who were killed in 1994.

killing of 10 Belgian UN peacekeepers, which led Belgium to withdraw all its troops. This left the way open for the army and militia to launch "death squads" into Tutsi communities, killing, looting, and burning wherever they went.

Every day for the next three months thousands of Tutsi and suspected Tutsi sympathizers were killed. Weapons ranged from sophisticated assault rifles to machetes and knives. Spurred on by radio and television, even women and children participated in the mass murder.

Within two days of the April 6 plane crash, the RPF launched a major offensive to stop the genocide. As they advanced, help from the UN did not come. The 2,500 UN troops in the country did not intervene because they were there as "monitors," not peacekeepers.

On July 4 the RPF captured Kigali, the capital. Now it was the turn of the Hutu to flee, mostly to Zaire (now called the Democratic Republic of the Congo). Two weeks later the RPF announced that the war had been won, a cease-fire was declared, and a broad-based Government of National Unity was formed.

WHEN THE WORLD TURNED AWAY

The genocide claimed between 800,000 and 1,000,000 lives. At the start of the killing there were 2,500 UN troops in Rwanda, but they made no attempt to stop the bloodshed. What went wrong?

One problem was that the slaughter took place between April and early July, a period of roughly three months. Although millions of people in other countries were shocked by the televised reports, it would have taken many weeks to mobilize a large enough force to stop the Hutu death squads.

Still, there is no question that the nations of the world, and their UN representatives, failed the people of Rwanda. The 2,500 UN soldiers had strict orders not to interfere and, when the 10 Belgians were killed, the UN force was reduced to an almost meaningless 250. On April 30 the UN Security Council discussed the crisis for eight hours but carefully avoided using the word "genocide." If the killings were labeled genocide, the UN would have been obliged to "prevent and punish" those responsible, according to the provisions of the Genocide Convention, written in response to the Holocaust, Nazi Germany's effort to destroy Europe's Jews. A decision in May to send 6,800 troops was delayed by debates over who would pay. By late August the UN troops began to arrive, and most governments recognized that genocide had taken place.

Rwandan refugees set up camp at Kibumba, Zaire (Congo) as civil war raged in their homeland.

THE AFTERMATH

Episodes of violence continued throughout the 1990s, and the roughly 2 million refugees crammed into camps in neighboring countries created a humanitarian crisis. Lack of food, clean water, and sanitary facilities led to disease, including a cholera epidemic at one camp that resulted in thousands of deaths.

The Government of National Unity, with Pasteur Bizimungu as president, took control in July 1994. Major General Paul Kagame was appointed defense minister and vice president. Over the next few years Kagame emerged as the real power in Rwanda. In March 2000 Bizimungu resigned, and Kagame was sworn in as president. He continued Rwanda's remarkable efforts to restore peace and stability and to end the ethnic strife.

In November 1994 the UN Security Council set up the International Criminal Tribunal for Rwanda (ICTR) to try those accused of genocide. By 1996, the year UN troops left Rwanda, the first suspects were on trial. In June 2002, however, there were still 115,000 genocide suspects in prison camps. To get the wheels of justice to turn more swiftly, the *gacaca* (ga-CHA-cha) judicial system was started to review lesser crimes.

GACACA

Gacaca is a traditional justice system devised by the Rwandan government to deal with the genocide suspects still in prison camps *(above)*. It was launched on June 18, 2002. It is enacted at the village level, and its goal is to bring to justice those accused of participating in the 1994 genocide.

This local court system takes its name from, and is modeled after, a traditional justice system of community hearings used to resolve local disputes. Over 250,000 judges, men and women elected by their own communities on the basis of their integrity, preside at hearings of prison detainees acused of genocide-related crimes. The system works by bringing the detainee back to the scene of the alleged crime. Local residents who witnessed the events are called upon to accuse or defend the person in an attempt to get at the truth of what happened.

Throughout Rwanda up to 11,000 *gacaca* courts are in operation. There is a panel of 19 judges per court; 15 judges and 100 witnesses are required for the court to be valid.

The government developed the *gacaca* system to deal with the backlog of genocide suspects. The hope is that this restorative justice system will help achieve unity and reconciliation in the country. In 2003 President Paul Kagame ordered the release of detainees who had already served time equal to the sentences they would have received if convicted. More than 22,000 prisoners were released in 2003 and another 4,500 in 2004. An additional 36,000 were freed to participate in *gacaca* hearings in July 2005.

Prisoners are freed to appear before *gacaca* courts. They then receive one month of training at solidarity camps, where they learn about Rwandan history, reconciliation, and justice.

RWANDA TODAY

Visitors to Rwanda express surprise and delight at the progress the country has made since those terrifying days in 1994. The international community, undoubtedly moved by a sense of guilt for ignoring the genocide, has also responded with many forms of assistance.

There is no denying that serious problems remain. Even the hard-won peace is not guaranteed, because thousands of Hutu refugees found protection in the Democratic Republic of the Congo (DRC), formerly called Zaire. After those Hutu refugees launched attacks on refugee camps located in Rwanda, a peace agreement was signed with

A graveyard memorial dedicated to the victims of the genocide.

the DRC. Rwandan leaders and the Tutsi people live with the awareness that ethnic violence could erupt again at any time.

One of the greatest successes of Rwanda's rebuilding has been the reduction of ethnic tension. After the genocide it would have been understandable if the RPF had launched a campaign of revenge. Instead, the approach has been one of reconciliation. This spirit of building unity helped persuade an estimated 2 million refugees to return to Rwanda. Identity cards, listing each Rwandan as Hutu, Tutsi, or Twa, have been discarded. The Hutu, who outnumber the Tutsi four to one, have so far accepted a government that seems dominated by the Tutsi. In 2003, when Rwanda's new constitution went into effect, the voters, including the Hutu majority, gave President Paul Kagame 3,544,777 votes, 95.05 percent of the total.

MEASURING THE EFFECTS OF THE GENOCIDE

In 1995 the United Nations Children's Fund (UNICEF) conducted "A National Trauma Survey" to estimate the percentage of children affected by the genocide in various ways. Here are some of their findings:

- 99.9 percent of children witnessed violence.
- 79.6 percent experienced death in the family.
- 69.5 percent witnessed someone being killed or injured.
- 61.5 percent were threatened with death.
- 90.6 percent had believed they would die.
- 57.7 percent witnessed killings or injuries with machetes.
- 87.5 percent saw dead bodies or parts of bodies.

GOVERNMENT

THE BASIC PROBLEM Rwanda faced after gaining independence on July 1, 1962, was finding a way to resolve the conflict between the two largest ethnic groups: the Hutu and the Tutsi. Government was one arena in which the two could try to find peaceful resolutions to their differences. Instead, each group tried to gain control of the government in order to dominate the other.

For the first three decades government activity reflected the Hutu majority's resolve to gain power. The constitution, adopted on November 24, 1962, established a presidential republic based on direct elections and universal adult suffrage (the right to vote). The president was the head of state and appointed a cabinet of ministers to head various departments. Both the president and a national assembly could introduce legislation. There was also an independent judiciary.

Left: **Paul Kagame, Rwanda's current president, is also the founder of the RPF.**

Opposite: **A soldier stands guard at the entrance of the presidential palace in Kigali.**

Grégoire Kayibanda was the first president of the new republic. He was a former teacher and a journalist for a Catholic newspaper. He was also the founder of a political party—PARMEHUTU (Party for the Emancipation of the Hutu People). Supported by the Hutu majority, he was reelected in 1965 and 1969.

HUTU DOMINANCE

Extremist elements among the Hutu were not satisfied. In July 1973, two months before the next election in which Kayibanda was to be the only candidate, the government was overthrown by the national guard, led by its commander Major General Juvénal Habyarimana. The National Assembly was dissolved, all political activity was outlawed, and Habyarimana was made the head of the government.

Over the next twenty years the Tutsi people, who had once dominated Rwanda, became an oppressed minority. Because thousands fled to neighboring countries, the remaining Tutsi made up only 9 percent of the population. They were now subject to strict quotas, such as being allowed no more than 9 percent of school positions and government appointments.

In 1975 Habyarimana's government formed a political party, the National Revolutionary Movement (MRND). Under a new constitution approved in 1978, this was the only legal party. Habyarimana was elected president under this new constitution and was reelected in 1983 and 1988.

During this period of Hutu dominance nothing was done to resolve the basic ethnic conflict. Tutsi refugees launched border raids, but these were easily quashed. During the same period a split developed among the Hutu, and the army came to be controlled by northerners eager to weaken the

Tutsi minority even further. However, when the new Rwandan Patriotic Front (RPF) invaded from Uganda in 1990–91, Habyarimana was forced to revise the constitution to allow other political parties, and he appointed some members of opposition parties to cabinet posts. This was a step toward a joint Hutu-Tutsi government, but the RPF wanted more.

THE GENOCIDE PERIOD

Following more violence between 1991 and 1993, a peace agreement was signed at Arusha, Tanzania, in August 1993. Both sides were to share power in a transitional government, and the army was to be integrated. After months of delay Habyarimana was installed as president in January 1994, but then was killed three months later when his plane was shot down at the Kigali airport.

Pictures of Habyarimana lie discarded on the front porch of the late president's home in Kigali. Habyarimana's wife, Agathe was airlifted out of Rwanda by French troops soon after the air crash.

Armed RPF soldiers in front of the Rwandan parliament building. The RPF managed to end the genocide after it defeated government forces led by Hutu extremists.

The genocide followed, with the extremist Hutu soldiers and militia determined to destroy the Tutsi people. When the violence was finally ended by the RPF, more than one-quarter of Rwanda's population had fled or been killed.

THE NEW RWANDAN GOVERNMENT

When the RPF took over in July 1994, the movement's leaders named two Hutu moderates to the transition government, with Pasteur Bizimungu as president and Faustin Twagiramungu as prime minister. Paul Kagame, leader of the RPF, became vice president. There were still roughly 2 million refugees, but these were now Hutu who feared that the RPF would seek revenge. Over the next five years, however, the government and the people worked hard at reconciliation rather than revenge and, by 2000, nearly all the Hutu refugees had returned.

After President Bizimungu and Prime Minister Twagiramungu resigned in 2000, Paul Kagame became the nation's fifth president. A new constitution

QUESTIONS OF FAIRNESS

In early 2004 foreign observers were shocked to learn that Pasteur Bizimungu (*above*), the former president of Rwanda, along with seven others, had been arrested and put on trial. A few weeks later Bizimungu was found guilty and sentenced to a prison term of fifteen years, five years each for civil disobedience, associating with criminal elements, and embezzlement of state funds. The other defendants received five-year sentences for criminal association.

Amnesty International immediately denounced the trials as a violation of Rwanda's constitution and criminal justice system in order to repress political opposition. "Through these actions," Amnesty International declared, "the Rwandese government is closing the door to any form of free and open political debate and discussion." Defense attorneys insist that none of the defendants were guilty of any of the activities of which they were accused.

The Rwandan government is equally insistent that the trials were fair and necessary. Officials say that the Commission for National Unity and Reconciliation continues to monitor the activities of individuals and groups that may try to undermine Rwanda's policy of unity and reconciliation. People throughout the world remain hopeful that the progress of the past 10 years will continue.

TORA
KAGAME Paul

Intwari iganisha u Rwanda aheza

INKINGI Y'UBUMWE
DEMOKARASI, N'AMAJYAMBERE

MASDJID
AL FATIH

A billboard urges Rwandans to vote for Paul Kagame in the 2003 presidential elections.

was approved in 2003, and in August the transition government was dissolved with the re-election of Kagame. A month later, the first post-genocide elections for the legislature were held. The next elections are scheduled for 2008.

Rwanda is still trying to escape its bloody past. In the past 10 years military forces have twice been involved in fighting in the Democratic Republic of the Congo (DRC). In mid-2005 there were still about 10,000 Hutu refugees living in the DRC, most of them armed and determined to regain control of Rwanda.

Some observers have begun to question the government's commitment to full equality for all cultural groups. There is evidence that the government is allowing less and less political dissent. Many outsiders were especially alarmed by the arrest, trial, and conviction of the former president and prime minister, Pasteur Bizimungu. They also argue that too much power is being concentrated in Kigali, with very little self-government being allowed in the local communities.

STRUCTURE OF THE GOVERNMENT

The constitution that was approved in June 2003 guarantees the basic civil rights of all citizens, bans the existence of political parties based on race, religion, or ethnic background, and expresses Rwanda's determination to eliminate ethnic conflict.

The three branches of government—executive, legislative, and judicial—are based on models from Western Europe and the United States.

The president is the head of state and is elected to a seven-year term by universal suffrage (all citizens age 18 and over are allowed to vote). A president cannot serve more than two terms. The president appoints a cabinet and a prime minister to oversee the carrying out, or execution, of national laws and policies.

A member of Rwanda's legislature, the Chamber of Deputies, takes an oath in a swearing-in ceremony held a few months after the PDF took over control of the government in 1994. Rwandans have since adopted a new national flag.

The legislative function is held by the National Assembly, which consists of two chambers: a Chamber of Deputies and a Senate. Of the 53 elected members of the Chamber of Deputies, 24 are women elected by provincial councils, two are chosen by the National Youth Council, and one by the Associations of the Disabled. All deputies serve five-year terms. The 26 members of the Senate serve eight-year terms. Twelve senators are elected by local councils, eight are appointed by the president, and six are selected by other groups. Thirty percent of the senators must be women. Most new pieces of legislation have to be passed by both chambers and then are signed into law by the president.

Rwanda's judicial system is modeled on the Belgian code of law combined with local laws and traditions. The highest court is the Supreme Court, consisting of 14 judges appointed for life by the Senate. The High Court of the Republic is below the Supreme Court, and both can hear appeals from local courts. A separate court in each local governmental unit considers both criminal and civil cases. The nation is divided into 11 provinces, each of which is divided into districts. The city of Kigali is a separate province.

WOMEN IN POLITICS

Since the genocide of 1994, women have greatly outnumbered men in Rwanda. Some estimate the ratio may be as high as seven to one. As the country rebuilds, women's voices are being heard more and more, and they are increasingly visible in politics. One result is that, of all the world's nations, Rwanda has the highest percentage of women (48.8 percent) in the lower, or popular, house of the National Assembly. Many women agreed with Athanasie Gahondogo (*above right, with her parliamentary colleagues*), a member of the Assembly, when she said, "I used to see politics as something bad, but now I also want a seat at the table."

Rwanda continues to be dominated by men in most respects, but the status of women is changing, and new laws being passed by the National Assembly are helping. Laws regarding inheritance, for example, have been made more liberal, which is helping to ease women's poverty. Odette Nyiramirimo, the head of the Senate Social Affairs and Human Rights Committee says, "We're learning fast because we have to." She has introduced a program to import donkeys. They will be bred and distributed to villages so that women's labor load will be reduced.

ECONOMY

IN MANY WAYS Rwanda seems to be a poor country with little chance of its citizens rising above the poverty levels that resulted from the 1994 genocide. The most crowded country in Africa must rely on agriculture in a desperate struggle to feed its growing population. Rwanda has little industry, few mineral resources, and a primitive transportation system. The legacy of the genocide includes a large number of widows and orphans and thousands of people suffering physical and psychological disabilities.

These negative factors are huge, but Rwanda has a number of valuable assets. The spectacular natural beauty of the country is one of those assets, including its primates, especially the famous mountain gorillas. The scenery and the wildlife have made tourism a major source of badly needed foreign dollars and one of Rwanda's great hopes for building a more prosperous economy.

Another great asset is the people. Since the nightmare of the mid-1990s, the Rwandan people have displayed remarkable courage, determination, and skill in rebuilding their ravaged population and in working to end ethnic hatred. Foreign observers say that, if Rwanda can continue the progress of the past ten years, its economy will soon reach and surpass pre-1994 levels.

Above: **A war widow and her children. Many women have had to fend for themselves after their husbands were killed during the genocide.**

Opposite: **The market remains the center of activity in Rwandan villages and towns.**

47

AGRICULTURE

Few countries in the world rely more heavily on agriculture than does Rwanda, with nearly 90 percent of its people engaged in farming. Most of the farming is subsistence agriculture, which means that a family produces enough to meet its own needs, with little or nothing left over to sell for profit.

A member of the Women's Agricultural Association. Many women were made widows as a result of the genocide, and they have had to take on the role of breadwinners for their families.

Because the country is so crowded, every available acre has to be producing food, even in the best of times. The genocide, however, left thousands of widows, many with young children, struggling to keep their family farms functioning. Those who could not manage slid into poverty.

By the late 1990s almost 60 percent of Rwanda's people lived below the officially established poverty line.

A farm family, with or without a male head, has to work hard on its small plot through two growing seasons, the first from September to January or February, the second from March to August. Farmers grow a wide variety of crops, including corn, bananas, beans, sorghum, potatoes, plantains, and soybeans.

Families are also now encouraged to use some of their land to grow one of Rwanda's important cash crops, either coffee or chrysanthemums. The flowers are used in the production of an insecticide called pyrethrum, which is one of the country's few sources of foreign income. Coffee is grown mostly on household farms (as well as on a few plantations). While coffee has also been an important cash crop, production declined 37 percent between 1990 and 2002—a decline that was caused more by a drop in world prices than by the genocide. There is considerable hope that new programs and foreign assistance have begun to reverse that decline. That hope is boosted by the exceptional quality of Rwanda's coffee beans.

A banana plantation. Bananas are one of the country's most economically important crops.

49

COFFEE: THE GREAT UNIFIER

For many years coffee ranked with tea as Rwanda's two most lucrative export crops. A drop in world prices combined with the chaos of the mid-1990s caused a huge loss in revenue. The government has responded with ambitious programs to revive the industry. One project is the Partnership for Enhancing Agriculture in Rwanda through Linkages, or PEARL. The key idea of PEARL is to help farmers learn a process for producing gourmet coffee by harvesting the ripest beans, then washing, sorting, and drying them at new community washing stations. One additional benefit of the program is that Hutu and Tutsi coffee growers are learning to work together.

Rwanda has an advantage in the world coffee market: the soil, hilly terrain, and cool climate produce outstanding strains. One variety, called Maraba Bourbon coffee, has been voted second best in the world in numerous international taste tests. As the coffee importer David Griswold has said, "Rwandan coffee has a nutty, fruity flavor you can't find anywhere else in the world."

Since 2001 PEARL has assisted eleven cooperatives with 15,000 members. In 2005 the Rwandan coffee harvest sold out, with international companies eagerly buying the uniquely flavored coffee beans.

Today the cooperatives are helping the country reunite, with Hutu and Tutsi farmers working side by side. Profits are growing, with the cooperatives' income jumping from $650,000 in 2004 to $1.2 million in 2005, and an expected $3 million in 2006.

A tea plantation near Ruhengeri.

Tea has long been Rwanda's most important cash crop. Most of the tea plantations are operated by a few major companies. Agricultural experts do not feel that increasing the number or size of tea plantations can add much to Rwanda's foreign earnings. They point out that in a typical year, such as 2002, Rwanda exported 15,000 tons of dried tea leaves, but the earnings on that amounted to only $18 million. The country needs far more in export earnings to offset the $250 million or more spent on imports each year.

The country's farm families have steadily increased the number of livestock animals they raise, especially since 2001. Cattle, sheep, and goats graze on open land and are kept in family compounds at night. In fact, the smaller ruminants (grazing animals) are proving increasingly popular. The goat population, for example, is rapidly catching up to the 815,000 cattle.

Workers at a brick-making factory in Butare.

INDUSTRIES AND MINING

Industries provide roughly 21 percent of the country's income, or gross domestic product (GDP), but their potential for growth is limited. Most manufacturing involves making products for local consumption, such as beverages, soap, furniture, shoes, a few plastic products, and textiles.

Although industry is growing at the rate of 7 percent a year, there is not much chance for exporting products to other countries for income. For one thing the country lacks the infrastructure for industrial expansion. For example, there are only 7,450 miles of road in the entire country, and not many of those miles are paved. Also, Rwanda has no railroads, although the roads do provide a link to the Uganda-Kenya railroad. The only way Rwanda can trade with distant lands is through Kenya's port of Mombasa, and getting products there is a cumbersome and expensive journey. Not only is international trade all but impossible, but domestic markets cannot expand much, either, particularly in light of the country's poverty. Foreign investors are more interested in commercial ventures, like financing facilities for tourism.

Mineral production contributes even less to the economy. Practically all the nation's mines were closed during the genocide. Since 1995 there has been a gradual reopening of some mines, and modest exports of gold, beryl, and tin have been renewed.

HANDICRAFT INDUSTRIES

An artisans' cooperative in Gisenyi.

Rwandan handicrafts offer one of Rwanda's best hopes for modest economic growth. Different groups have preserved traditional crafts, including making pottery, carving wood, and weaving baskets, mats, and wall hangings. Some also show great skill making musical instruments, beadwork, and jewelry. If tourism continues to grow, sales of local items should increase dramatically.

International organizations, recognizing this potential, have begun to establish self-help projects. The Pottery Project, for example, is part of a larger British-funded program to help the Batwa (the Twa's name for themselves) improve their pottery and the marketing of it. These forest people, as they are called, have developed new techniques and styles, and the project has helped them develop new marketing strategies, such as bringing tourists to their studios and retail outlets. After starting with six groups of potters, the project has steadily expanded.

FISHERIES

Fishing has been a small but valuable industry for many years, operated by local cooperatives (groups of several fisher families) on lakes Kivu, Cyohoha, and Mugasera. During the genocide, however, and for several years after, the lakes were not adequately restocked, so the output declined steadily. Growing support for fish farms is helping to revive the industry. In addition, old fishing ponds have been upgraded, and new ones are being opened.

Fishermen pull trawl nets out of a river.

TRADE AND FINANCE

Even though nearly 90 percent of the people are engaged in farming, Rwanda still has to import some food products. In addition, the country needs to buy a wide variety of products from other countries, including machinery, motor vehicles, and clothing. Like many developing nations Rwanda's exports do not earn the nation enough to offset the cost of these imports, which amounts to about $265 million per year. This trade imbalance can force the government deeper into debt every year.

The years of ethnic strife have added to Rwanda's financial plight. For the first two decades of independence—from 1962 to 1980—the country's GDP had grown at a healthy rate of 6.5 percent each year, then dropped to under 3 percent from 1980–85. As the ethnic conflict began, the economy became stagnant, and then its growth rate dropped every year from the late 1980s through 1994. And in 1994, the year of the genocide, the GDP declined by a staggering 40 percent. These cold statistics, translated into human terms, mean that the country and the people were becoming desperately poor.

The decline in Rwanda's finances is reflected in the currency—the Rwandan franc. In 1999, 334 Rwandan francs equaled one U.S. dollar; by 2004, 575 were needed to buy one U.S. dollar.

The fact that Rwanda has been able to reverse the decline in GDP reflects the energy and ability of its people. Peace was established in late 1994, and the GDP grew by 9.5 percent the following year. The growth rate has been about 5 percent each year since then. Each individual's share of the nation's GDP translates into purchasing power estimated at $1,300 per year per person.

These figures on international trade and finance are indicators of how much Rwanda must do to regain a measure of prosperity.

The international community has already offered some help through the International Monetary Fund's decision that Rwanda is eligible for debt relief. This means that the government will have more money to spend on improvements.

FACING THE FUTURE

Early in the new century the Kigali government established goals for the future: The Millennium Development Goals and Visions 2020. One of the main goals is "to eradicate extreme poverty and hunger." More specifically the goals state that the proportion of people living below the poverty line "should not exceed 23.8 percent." That would be about half the 1990 level.

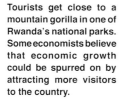

Tourists get close to a mountain gorilla in one of Rwanda's national parks. Some economists believe that economic growth could be spurred on by attracting more visitors to the country.

One obvious path to economic expansion is achieving growth in foreign tourism, tea exports, and coffee exports. If Rwanda can maintain peace and stability, there's a good chance for growth in all three sectors. The production and marketing of tea had been controlled by a government agency that is now disbanded, and the industry is being privatized (turned over to private companies) under the supervision of a tea board.

While the increase in revenue from tea and coffee production will depend on the world market, the government, often supported by international agencies, is trying to expand other agricultural areas. Some of these efforts, like growing flowers and vegetables for sale in foreign cities, have been slowed by the nation's poor transportation system. Several international agencies are now providing grants to improve existing roads and build new ones. Some new agricultural products that do not require fast shipment, including macadamia nuts, plums, and passion fruit, are already increasing earnings for many families.

Foreign economists agree that Rwanda's best hope for significant economic growth lies in improving tourism. Some international agencies and even more private companies have begun investing in services for tourists, including resort hotels and improved facilities and trails in all the parks and national forests. A number of licensed agencies offer guided gorilla treks, following strict regulations to avoid harming these huge, gentle creatures in any way. Veterans of these treks agree that it is one of the most memorable wildlife experiences in Africa, which suggests its potential for contributing to Rwanda's economy.

Even the efforts of small, nonprofit organizations are boosting Rwanda's economy, often in ways that boost morale as well as earning power. The Send-a-Cow Foundation, for example, began sending smaller farm animals to families with orphans and providing instruction to help young

A Rwandan farmstead. With the end of the genocide, one of the most pressing needs is the development of the agriculture sector. Most Rwandans are totally dependent on the land for their necessities.

people learn to care for rabbits, goats, and other small livestock. Cows were sent to farms that had enough land, and more than 300 have been distributed in the past 10 years.

Small, grassroots organizations include several Rwandan nonprofit agencies. One of these, CICODEB, has helped more than 200 farm groups with technical assistance as well as farm animals and improved seeds. Another Rwandan agency operated by the country's Presbyterian Church provides job-training workshops for street children in Kigali. The students learn a wide variety of skills, from cutting hair to making furniture.

Rwandans insist that the Rwanda of today is not the country of the mid-1990s. They point with pride to the many signs of growing prosperity. If they can maintain the stability and progress of the past 10 years, the country will be known for more than the horror of genocide.

SELF-HELP FOR WOMEN

In August 1994, when the killing stopped, an organization of women was formed. Known as Association de Solidarite des Femmes Rowandaises (ASOFERWA), the organization was dedicated to helping those left alone and vulnerable by the genocide—widows, orphans, teenage mothers, victims of AIDS (through rape), and those psychologically traumatized by the genocide. The organization helped with the government's establishment of "peace villages." Each village contains 100 to 150 houses, with a population of 600 to 1,200. Widows who were rehoused in the villages were asked to take in orphans and raise them. ASOFERWA also helped the women set up income-producing schemes, such as farms, handicrafts workshops, and small shops.

International agencies have provided funds for expansion, helping ASOFERWA to set up schools, training centers, a tannery, and a modern dairy farm. One of the most recent ventures is the establishment of Kinigi Guest House *(above)*, a resort at the entrance to Volcanoes National Park.

ENVIRONMENT

POVERTY AND HUNGER are two great enemies of the environment. People whose daily lives are filled with the gnawing of hunger will destroy portions of their surrounding environment rather than starve. They will allow their livestock to overgraze the land, sacrificing next year's grass so that the animals can stay alive this year. And they will cut down the last tree in order to have fuel to cook their food or heat their homes.

These actions are only natural, but such survival instincts serve people only in the short term. The poor or the starving do not need to be lectured about how important it is to protect the environment for the future. For them the only future is getting through today.

Rwanda shares this dilemma with every other poor nation. How can the country's leaders persuade people to plant trees or preserve wetlands or avoid overgrazing when their immediate needs are so urgent? But they must be persuaded. Economists and environmentalists agree that a country such as Rwanda can achieve a decent standard of living only if it has a solid environmental protection program in place.

DEFORESTATION

The loss of forests is one of Rwanda's most urgent environmental problems, and it is connected to other serious problems. Entire forests have been leveled, especially over the past half century. Large areas of forest have been destroyed to create more land for growing crops or for grazing animals. Forests have also been leveled for timber and firewood.

Population pressure has caused a steady reduction in size in all of the country's forested areas. The Nyungwe Forest in the southwest of Rwanda has probably suffered the least, partly because the Belgian government made it a protected reserve in 1933. Only about 20 percent of the forest was lost over the 50 years that followed.

Opposite: **A waterfall in Nyungwe National Park. Rwanda's natural beauty is being threatened by deforestation and poaching.**

Nyungwe remains the only large tract of forest left in Rwanda. The Gishwati Forest, which was about the same size as Nyungwe in the 1930s, was reduced to two separate blocks covering 174 square miles (280 square km) by 1989; since then most of those two blocks have been broken up for cropland and pasture.

Nowhere has the pressure of population been so dramatic than in the Akagera National Park region on Rwanda's eastern border with Tanzania. Much of the park remains the kind of savanna ecosystem seen in movies, with lions, leopards, and other predators following large herds of antelope, buffalo, zebra, and elephant. In addition, the region's six lakes and wetlands are home to one of the largest hippopotamus populations in Africa, as well as Nile crocodiles. But the need for farmland has led to a drastic shrinking of the park, especially after the genocide, when many of the 3 million returning refugees were given land. In 1998 alone the total area of the park was reduced by almost two-thirds, from 617,300 to 222,200 acres (250,000 to 90,000 ha). Much of the remaining parkland is used for fishing camps and cattle grazing.

The Rwandan government and environmental groups are trying to persuade the people that preserving Akagera's forests and wetlands is in their own interest. Government agents educate farm families by showing how the loss of forestland seriously limits their chances for a better life.

THE RIPPLE EFFECT

Damage to one part of an ecosystem has a ripple effect through all parts of the system. Deforestation, for example, often leads to soil erosion. Rain washes away precious soil, making it less productive for growing crops. More serious effects can be disastrous floods or landslides. The danger of landslides is especially great in hilly areas, because farm families move in as soon as the trees are gone and plant crops without knowing how to terrace the land. Government agricultural agents are trying to reduce this danger by showing farm families the value of terraced farming to slow water and soil runoff.

Deforested tracts of land are prone to flooding.

"People in different parts of the country have been buried alive and others drowned. Whole farms and homesteads have been swept away, with great loss of life and property."

—Ugirashebuja Emmanuel, researcher in environmental Law, on landslides and floods resulting from deforestation

63

Deforestation also has long-term effects, including climate change. The loss of forests leads to a reduction in rainfall, with less moisture collecting in lakes, ponds, and wetlands. Over time this produces a warmer, drier climate.

Another long-term effect of deforestation is the loss of biodiversity. One of Rwanda's great treasures is the amazing variety of plant and animal life it contains. When a forest ecosystem is reduced or destroyed, some species will die out, while animals may migrate to other forested areas. The loss of forest, savanna, and wetlands in Akagera National Park has already led many groups of large mammals to move east into Tanzania. Akagera's elephant population has declined dramatically over the past 10 years, for example, to a total of about 60. Environmentalists point out that this herd, centered around Lake Hugo, can expand rapidly if the park is preserved and the animals are protected from poachers. Clearly, Rwanda's hopes of attracting tourists can be severely limited by further loss of habitat.

WETLANDS

A swamp near Kigali.

The pressure of rapid population growth has also led to the dramatic loss of wetlands. Currently, more than half of Rwanda's wetlands are used for agriculture. Farm families use the swampy areas to grow such crops as rice, and the drier regions to grow such crops as vegetables and sugarcane.

The growth of urban areas has added to wetland damage. Building construction, for example, requires wetland resources, including sand. In addition, some industries have built on wetlands to make use of those resources, while other businesses have been dumping toxic waste into the wetlands. Even handicraft industries, such as mat and basket weaving, place an additional burden on wetland resources for raw materials.

Perhaps the greatest danger to the wetlands is the draining of large areas to create land for new settlements and for crops. Draining wetlands means that less water is flowing into streams. In some areas springs have dried up, and groundwater is very low. As in the case of deforestation, the shrinking of wetlands contributes to a loss of biodiversity. The protection of both wetlands and forests has become a major 21st-century priority for Rwanda's government and private organizations.

RWANDA'S ENVIRONMENTAL PROGRAM

Over the past 10 years the Rwandan government has implemented an ambitious program of environmental protection, combining strict laws to reduce damage with projects that will enable Rwandans to gain immediate benefits from conservation. The government has received a good deal of financial and technical help from environmental agencies in Rwanda and from international organizations, including the UN and the World Bank.

Here are some examples of current environmental protection programs. With volunteer labor and financial help from international organizations, more than 10 million seedlings have been planted as part of a reforestation program. In addition to these plantings along roads and on private farms, the government has reforested roughly 9,880 acres (4,000 ha) of land. To protect the trees from disease, a variety of species are planted, including eucalyptus, lemon, and acacia. This program works especially well when combined with programs to provide alternatives to wood for cooking fuel, such as programs that provide solar-powered ovens.

New laws have been passed to reduce the degradation of both forests and wetlands. For example, a new agency, Rwanda Environmental Management Authority (REMA), has control over all use of wetlands; any new wetland activity requires written approval from REMA.

Two young chimpanzees poached from Volcanoes National Park await their release after being rescued by the Rwandan authorities.

Wherever possible, the government tries to combine environmental protection programs with profit-making programs. As in all urban areas, for example, Rwanda faced a serious problem with the disposing of solid wastes, especially in Kigali and other population centers. This posed a great threat to delicate wetland ecosystems. With technical assistance from the Kigali Institute of Science, Technology and Management (KIST), several women's associations have established special dump sites where they process garbage into fertilizers and household cooking fuels. Garbage has become a money-making proposition for the women, and Kigali has gained a reputation as a remarkably clean capital city.

Forest rangers on the trail of poachers in Volcanoes National Park. Wildlife conservation is an integral part of Rwanda's effort to attract more tourists.

A silverback gorilla in Volcanoes National Park.

SAVING THE GORILLAS

Some foreign journalists have questioned the wisdom of devoting so much money to protecting mountain gorillas, when more than half the country's people live in poverty.

The people of Rwanda have come to understand that their future is intimately connected with the future of a few hundred mountain gorillas. The survival of these remaining gorillas is likely to depend on tourism, since tourists' dollars provide the income needed to stop poaching and preserve the mountain habitat. The future health of Rwanda's economy, in turn, is largely dependent on the revenue and jobs generated by tourism.

Several international organizations are helping the Rwandan government protect the gorillas and expand tourism. Laws that combine public education and economic development projects with restrictions help promote environmental protection. Experienced beekeepers are forbidden from operating within Volcanoes National Park, for example, but they are given aid to establish honey farms on the park's edge. Similarly, schoolchildren who used to fill their family water jugs at springs inside the park now collect it from village water cisterns. Schools provide conservation courses for students of all ages, including field trips and ideas for exploring links with schools in other countries.

KEEPING TRACK OF THE MOUNTAIN GORILLA

During the civil war years park rangers and researchers were forced to evacuate Volcanoes National Park, and the area was part of an escape route used by thousands of refugees trying to flee the slaughter. There was concern that many of the gorillas would not survive because poachers were still active in all of Rwanda's parks and because of the spread of disease from humans to gorillas. Trophy collectors paid high prices for gorilla heads and hands, which were used as ashtrays!

Researchers had kept careful track of the four gorilla groups in the park and were familiar with most of the nearly 300 individuals. When researchers were finally able to return to the park, they were amazed to discover that only four of the gorillas could not be accounted for. Poachers did kill seven gorillas in 1995. Still the low numbers that were killed rekindles the hope that the gorilla population will survive and increase in number (Mountain gorillas have never reproduced in captivity). And, of course, a healthy, growing gorilla population is vital for the nation's tourism industry.

RWANDANS

WHEN RWANDA EXPLODED into civil war and then the genocide of 1994, people in the United States and other countries were puzzled by the early TV-news accounts of "death squads" roaming the countryside, brutally murdering men, women, and children. Who was doing the killing and who were the victims? Why were Rwandans killing each other? (The TV reports stopped abruptly when the news crews fled with the UN troops.)

Many Rwandans were also bewildered. They could not understand the wholesale slaughter that made victims of even the youngest children. In spite of tensions between the Hutu and the Tutsi, there was a widespread belief that ethnic differences could be overcome. After all, there was a good deal of intermarriage between the two groups, so how could one group try to destroy the other? The victims themselves often had no idea why they were being attacked. One often-repeated account of the genocide tells of a group of schoolgirls who were told by a death squad to divide into Hutu and Tutsi, with the understanding that Hutu would be spared. But the girls refused to divide, insisting instead that they were all Rwandans. They were all murdered.

What led to such blind rage? How could members of the death squads convince themselves that they were justified in butchering every Tutsi in sight and any Hutu who seemed sympathetic toward them? The seeds of some of the hatred were planted as far back as 500 years ago.

THE HUTU AND TUTSI

Nearly 90 percent of Rwanda's population of 8,440,820 (2004 estimate) are Hutu and about 9 percent are Tutsi. (A third group, the small-statured Twa, make up less than 1 percent of the population.) Both the Hutu and the Tutsi are Bantu-speaking groups who share a common culture and language.

Opposite: **A Tutsi woman at a market.**

Hutu and Tutsi children doing their schoolwork together in Akagera. National reconciliation is integral to the Rwandan government's efforts to prevent a repeat of the violence that erupted in 1994.

Of the two main groups the Hutu arrived in the region first, beginning around 700 B.C. or even earlier. Throughout history most Hutu were farmers, growing crops and raising some livestock—goats, sheep, and some cattle.

Because Rwanda has no written history, it is impossible to say when the Tutsi first arrived or where they came from. From the oral tradition of the people, historians can tell that the Tutsi were present in large numbers by the 16th century. Unlike the agricultural Hutu, the Tutsi were nomadic pastoralists, or herders, who relied on their cattle for food.

The Tutsi quickly gained power over the Hutu and dominated the feudal system called *ubuhake*. In the *ubuhake* system wealth and the power of being an overlord or master were based on the number of cattle owned. The Tutsi herders, being cattle owners, were often in positions of power, although the Hutu, and even some Twa, could acquire cattle by purchase, by war, or by marriage. With this system firmly in place, the Tutsi formed a dominant class similar to the nobility of Europe, and the Hutu were a large underclass of peasant farmers. People could switch positions—Hutu could join the Tutsi class and vice versa, but this was not common.

By the 20th century there were other modifications to the *ubuhake* system. A number of Tutsi worked in business or in government posts. And the king, or *mwami*, was invariably Tutsi. And some Hutus left farming to work in towns, and some became ceramists (potters).

Although this feudal system placed the Hutu in a position of almost permanent inferiority, there was little evidence of rebellion. Intermarriage was not uncommon. Any Hutu resentment seems to have been repressed until the 20th century, when the period of German and Belgian rule brought points of friction into the open.

THE EUROPEAN INFLUENCE

Rwanda was part of Germany's colonial empire for less than 20 years, but this was long enough to expose the tension between the Hutu and Tutsi. In 1911 and 1912 the Germans joined with the Tutsi monarchy to conquer two Hutu areas in the north. The Hutu were proud of their independence and fought vigorously before being forced to surrender. Their resentment seethed until after independence was achieved in 1962.

Belgium took control of the two areas that became Rwanda and Burundi in 1916 and, in 1919, Belgium was entrusted with the area as a League of Nations mandate. After World War II (1939–45) and the creation of the UN, Ruanda-Urundi became a UN Trust Territory. Belgium had become a major colonial power in Africa in the 19th century and controlled the much larger Belgian Congo to the west. The Belgians had a strict program for "civilizing" colonial peoples and they applied these ideas to Rwandans between 1916 and 1962, when Rwanda became an independent nation.

During the nearly half century of Belgian rule the Europeans had considerable success in improving physical aspects of the colony. For example, teams of agricultural specialists fanned out across Rwanda and

A Twa mother and her child in Gishwati. In the past the Twa were favored by the Tutsi nobility for their pottery and dance skills.

showed farm families how to increase production by using improved seeds and chemical fertilizers. Most important, they taught the Hutu men and women how to shape hillsides into terraces to avoid disastrous soil erosion. In terms of human relations, however, the Belgians inadvertently fed the simmering tensions between the Hutu and the Tutsi. They undermined the authority of the *mwami* by using Belgian officials instead of his trusted Tutsi administrators. Then, following a 1948 UN report critical of the low status of the Hutu and the Twa, more attention was paid to providing opportunities for the Hutu.

In the 1950s the Hutu themselves began demanding a stronger voice in government, and in 1954 the *ubuhake* system was officially abolished. At the same time the Catholic Church became a major supporter of the Hutu and encouraged them to become involved in the political process. Quite suddenly the Belgians, who had always supported the powerful Tutsi minority, switched their loyalty to the Hutu.

Once independence was achieved and the Hutu majority controlled the government, Rwanda's two main ethnic groups experienced a great role reversal. After dominating the society, economy, and government for several hundred years, the Tutsi became a virtually powerless minority. And the Hutu, formerly regarded as a lower class, were now determined to solidify their dominance. The Tutsi were to be limited to 9 percent of positions in schools, businesses, and government, reflecting the fact that they accounted for that percentage of the population. To make this quota system work, the Hutu relied on one of the legacies of Belgian rule: identity cards that stated whether the cardholder was Hutu, Tutsi, or of mixed ethnicity.

THE TWA

The Twa, once called Pygmies, a term now considered to be derogatory, are believed to be the descendants of the original residents of what is now Rwanda. Today they number only about 25,000, less than 1 percent of the total population. The Twa, or Batwa as they call themselves, lived for centuries as hunters and gatherers. When the Hutu moved in and established farms, the Twa moved onto mountain slopes and into forests.

During the period of the Rwandan kingdoms, the Twa were favored in the royal court. Many emerged from the forests to become potters. Some also became dancers at the royal court. They became famous for a dance they performed with Tutsi dancers.

Because of their small stature, the Twa have suffered a great deal of prejudice. They have usually been regarded as inferior and have lived in extreme poverty. Even today, many have to beg to survive. Only 28 percent of Twa children go to primary school, compared with 95 percent for the general population, and far fewer even start secondary school. They also suffered severely during the genocide: an estimated 30 percent were killed, compared with 14 percent of the population overall.

A survivor of the 1994 mass murder wrote, "Before the genocide, Hutus and Tutsis lived together. I remember we used to play with Hutu children and share everything. There were even intermarriages. The only time we felt discriminated against was when a place at school, or a job, was given to a Hutu, even if there was a Tutsi more qualified for it. But this was no reason for hatred between the two groups."

—Quoted in Philip Gourevitch, We Wish to Inform You that Tomorrow We Will Be Killed with Our Families, 1998.

Cheering Rwandan fans wave national flags at a soccer match between Ethiopia and Rwanda at Kigali Stadium in 2005. The government under Kagame has striven to break down the ethnic differences that resulted in the bloodshed of the past through appealing to Rwandans' shared heritage.

RWANDANS TODAY

Since 1995 the Rwandan people have been committed to overcoming the stereotypes concerning ethnic differences that led to conflict and violence. The statement of the Rwanda Embassy in Washington, D.C. emphasizes the sameness of the people without mentioning the differences:

> Inhabitants of Rwanda are called 'Banyarwanda.' They speak the same language, have the same culture, live on the same hills and, for centuries, have intermarried. The three 'ethnic' groups are the Bahutu, the Batutsi, and the Batwa, referred to in the West as Hutus, Tutsis, and Twas.

In schools and on public occasions, people emphasize the unity. In 2003, for example, when the Rwandan soccer team beat the highly regarded Ghanaian team 1 to 0 to qualify for the 2004 African Nations Cup, there was great celebrating in the streets of Kigali that lasted all day and all night. Observers could not distinguish between Hutu or Tutsi either among the celebrants or the players.

Problems have not disappeared completely, of course. News reports of discrimination or prejudice are common, and international organizations report some abuses. But so far these rough spots in the road have not dampened people's confidence in Rwanda's peaceful future.

Far from turning away from Rwanda, international organizations continue to provide important support, often with the goal of promoting unity and understanding. The Forest People's Project (FPP), funded by a British organization, works with the Twa to bring them into the mainstream of the society and economy. A number of organizations focus on providing help for Rwandan women, especially widows and other victims of the genocide. In addition, the Government of National Unity has worked with women's organizations to encourage girls to go to school. Although education historically has been a low priority for girls, by 2003 as many girls as boys were enrolled in primary school, and the proportion continuing to secondary school is now close to the same.

MEASURING DIFFERENCES

In the early 1900s some Europeans engaged in a pseudoscience called eugenics to categorize racial and ethnic groups according to physical characteristics, such as height, bone structure, and coloring, in order to improve and rank the quality of races. It was this pseudoscience that led the leaders of Nazi Germany to describe Germans as a "superior race," while other groups, such as Jews, Slavs, and Roma (once known by the non-derogatory term "Gypsies"), were deemed inferior. In Rwanda first the Germans and then the Belgians were struck by physical differences between the Hutu and Tutsi. The Twa, of course, were even easier to identify because of their short stature. The Europeans had noticed that the Tutsi tended to be quite tall, often over 6 feet, and well proportioned. The Hutu, on the other hand, were usually shorter and squatter.

In the early 1930s the Belgians launched a census to categorize all Rwandans. Many people, especially the Hutu, felt humiliated by "scientists," armed with calipers, measuring tapes, scales, and charts, spending hours measuring them from head to toe. When a clear categorization could not be made because intermarriage had led to an ethnic blending, the census taker made a judgment. If the person seemed well educated or prosperous, he or she was labeled Tutsi.

In 1935 the Belgian government issued identity cards for all Rwandans. These identity cards became standard from that time on. While the cards did not have a major influence on the genocide in 1994, they were one more indicator of who would be killed and who would be spared.

LIFESTYLE

EVERYDAY LIFE in Rwanda suffered massive disruption during the civil war and genocide, and much of the past decade has been a time of rebuilding. Rebuilding has involved restoring houses, businesses, and even entire villages and towns. Much of the capital city, Kigali, was destroyed during the genocide. Workers in businesses and government offices returned in late 1994 to find office machines wrecked and tons of files destroyed or strewn in all directions.

More important, the rebuilding has involved restoring a way of life. The survivors of the genocide could not simply return to traditional family life. Too many families had been torn apart. Instead, widows and orphans have had to reconstruct families, older children often becoming "parents" to younger siblings.

In spite of the upheaval most Rwandans seem to go about the task of reconstructing their lives with that surprising energy and hope that has characterized all aspects of life in the postwar years. Government agencies and international organizations have provided various kinds of assistance.

Above: **Most rural Rwandans live in *rugos*, homesteads consisting of circular-shaped houses with thatched roofs.**

Opposite: **An eager student raises his hand to answer a teacher's question. As Rwandans begin the long process of reconstructing their country, it is only through educating the young that they will be able to secure the nation's future.**

RURAL LIFE

Nearly 90 percent of the Rwandan people live in rural areas. The typical rural community is usually not a defined village, such as those found in rural America. Instead, most people live in a *rugo*, a traditional homestead consisting of several beehive-shaped houses within a larger family compound. These family compounds, in turn, are scattered over the seemingly endless hills that make up the landscape of Rwanda.

A small rural village in Burera. Most Rwandans live in the countryside.

The most important family house, usually the home of a respected elder, is in the middle of the compound. The traditional houses are made of woven branches and grasses, covered with smooth clay. Windows and doors are set in wooden frames. In the 21st century modern Western-style houses have become more common, although the layout of the compounds remains the same. Each house is surrounded by a fence, usually made of thick bushes.

In Kinyarwanda, the language of Rwanda, the word *inzu* can refer to a family, a household, or a house. The term usually means a husband and wife, their children, and other close relatives. Large families are common, and a family without children is thought to be incomplete, an object of pity. When people from several *inzu* can trace their origins to a common male ancestor, they form a kinship unit called an *umuryango*, which is led by the oldest and most respected male.

LIFE IN KIGALI

Kigali was a small farm town until Rwanda gained independence in 1962. As the country prepared for independence most people thought Butare would be named the capital, since it had been the administrative center of Rwanda during Belgian rule. Kigali was chosen instead, probably because of its central location, and that choice led to explosive growth. From a town of a few thousand, Kigali had a population of more than half a million people by 2005, making it the only real city in Rwanda.

The city was originally built on a ridge and now extends down both hillsides to the valley floors and onto a second ridge. Kigali today is remarkably neat and clean, the streets lined with flowering trees and shrubs. Although heavily damaged in 1994, much of it has been rebuilt, and a construction boom has been underway since the late 1990s. Visitors say that the residents, including returning refugees, are very forward-looking. As a UN worker said, "People would rather talk about their plans than their past."

The business and social center of the city is colorful, noisy, and bustling with activity. The pace slows down for an hour or two in the early afternoon. Foreign and Rwandan businesspeople dressed in business attire share the crowded streets with Rwandans dressed in traditional clothing or in casual Western-style clothes. Young boys earn a little money by hawking newspapers and audio cassettes. Elderly men sit at rickety desks on street corners equipped with battered old typewriters, ready to type letters dictated by the many illiterate Rwandans. A few upscale

Construction workers hard at work on the building site of a South African bank in Kigali. The capital has experienced a construction boom since the PDF-led government began its reconstruction efforts.

A busy street in Kigali. The lifestyles of urban dwellers contrast greatly with those living in the countryside.

restaurants cater to Rwandan businesspeople and the many representatives of international agencies.

A newer section of the city, located on another hill, houses government and administrative offices. Many of the buildings display striking 21st-century architecture, much of it designed by Rwandan architects. The tempo there is decidedly more quiet and sedate.

Tree-lined residential streets extend down the hills. Many of the houses look more like modern houses in Europe or America.

VARIATIONS IN URBAN LIFESTYLES

Kigali is the only large city in Rwanda. The next largest, Butare, with fewer than 100,000 people is often called the intellectual center of Rwanda, largely because it is the site of the National University of Rwanda. The pace of life is slower than in Kigali, in spite of it being a university town. The marketplace, where vendors sell all sorts of clothing, hardware, and foods, is busy, crowded, and noisy. It is also full of the sound of drums from the performances or practices of traditional dance troupes.

Butare is also the home of the National Museum of Rwanda, which houses displays on Rwandan history and culture. The museum, which opened in 1988, was a gift from the king of Belgium to celebrate the country's independence. It is regarded as the best museum in East Africa for its presentation of geological and historical information.

Other towns in Rwanda serve mostly as administrative centers. Some house foreign visitors working with various aid organizations. A number of towns, such as Gikongoro and Gisenyi, are gaining new businesses designed to attract and serve tourists. A few others, such as Kibuye and Cyangugu, on Lake Kivu, serve as fishing ports and beach towns.

Traditional woven baskets on display at the National Museum of Rwanda in Butare.

A market in Byumba. For rural communities, market days are highlights of the social calendar.

VARIATIONS IN RURAL LIFESTYLES

Most Rwandan families live by farming. The majority barely eke out an existence. Daily life is a struggle to get enough food from the basic crops grown and the small livestock (primarily goats and sheep) raised. Cattle are raised, mostly by the Tutsi, but as symbols of wealth and status rather than for food. Most Rwandans eat meat only two or three times a month. Their basic diet consists of vegetables, fruit, and grain (such as millet or corn).

Many rural people combine making handicrafts with raising crops to make a living. The Twas, for example, are famous for their pottery. Others, both Hutu and Tutsi, are wood carvers, while still others make furniture, fabrics, or musical instruments.

Clothing styles are slowly changing as low-cost European and American designs become more readily available. Many people continue to prefer traditional clothing, men in loose-fitting white garments and women in brightly colored wraps.

Fridays are market days in Rwandan villages and administrative centers. Stalls offer a striking array of merchandise, including cattle, sheep, goats, and pigs, as well as vegetables, fruits, clothing, and housewares. There are stacks of mattresses with bright, floral-print covers, recycled pots and pans, and handmade unpainted furniture. Boom boxes blare loud music, both African and American. The activity is colorful and lively, and the market offers people the chance to see old friends and make new ones.

MARRIAGE AND FAMILY

The family is central to Rwandan life, so it is expected that every woman will marry. (Only about 1 woman in 200 reaches her 40s without marrying.) When a couple wishes to marry, the groom's family first pays a bride-price to the bride's father, usually giving a cow or other livestock. A couple can dissolve a marriage if both agree and if the bride-price is returned to the groom's family. Over the past 30 or 40 years, couples have been marrying later, often in their 30s. The delay is usually because the couple does not have land for starting a farm, or else the groom cannot afford the bride-price.

Other family traditions have also given way to the pressures of modern life. In the past, for example, after a child was born, both the mother and infant remained in seclusion for eight days. On the day they reentered family life, relatives gave presents to the new parents, and the baby was introduced to the family. When the infant was 3 or 4 months old, a naming ceremony was held. Only the most traditional families continue these practices.

CREATIVE LIFESTYLES

The loss of life in the 1994 genocide caused thousands of Rwandans to face the challenge of reconstructing families and jobs. Many widows, aided and encouraged by international agencies, created households consisting of three or more women and up to a dozen orphans.

Outside the town of Nyabisindu, four women, all widows, established the Oakdale Demonstration Farm. They use milk from their own cows to make cheddar cheese, usually sold in large wheels. Other farmers can sell their milk to the farm, as long as it passes purity tests. The women also raise turkeys and pigs. In 2005 work began on building and stocking fishponds.

EDUCATION

Education in the primary grades is free, and officially at least, it is compulsory for children ages 7 through 12. In reality, however, enrollment never reaches 100 percent, although it has been close to perfect since 2001.

Secondary and technical school enrollment has not kept pace, however, with only about 14 percent of eligible students enrolled. The low secondary school enrollment is reflected in another statistic: only 70.4 percent of adults are literate (able to read and write).

Many Rwandans are aware of the vital role education plays in building a modern nation. Education at all levels was hit hard during the 1990s,

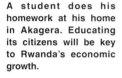

A student does his homework at his home in Akagera. Educating its citizens will be key to Rwanda's economic growth.

when most schools and the university closed their doors. It was not until 1995 or later that primary and secondary schools began to reopen. The National University of Rwanda in Butare opened in 1963 and had about 2,500 students in 1990. After being shut down for much of the decade, the university is gradually getting back to normal. There are 4,500 students enrolled today and a faculty of 275. Thousands of teachers and students were killed in the genocide, and Rwanda has had difficulty finding enough qualified teachers. Volunteers from other countries have helped fill the gaps.

Language has added a complicating factor. The spoken language of Rwanda is Kinyarwanda, a Bantu language, but the official written languages are French and English. Instruction has to be provided in two languages (French and English), providing an extra burden on teachers and students. Students have to take a language examination in order to graduate.

A new institution of higher eduation is the Kigali Institute of Science, Technology, and Management (KIST). Opened in 1997, KIST held its first graduation ceremony in 2002. The new institution provides an ambitious array of programs: The Faculty of Technology offers education in engineering, food sciences, and business, including small-scale, or "cottage" industries. The Faculty of Science provides only introductory courses in mathematics, chemistry, and physics, with further study needed outside the country. The Centre for Continuing Education has part-time courses in such subjects as computers and languages.

A unique feature of the Kigali Institute is the African Virtual University. Founded in 1999 with financing by the World Bank, the university provides distance-learning courses in electronics, engineering, computer science, and business management. In addition, KIST has a Centre for Innovations and Technology, which is designed to help people in rural areas learn

An aid worker attends to a sick refugee in Rwanda. After helping with the most immediate problems stemming from the genocide, many non-government agencies have stayed on to help rebuild Rwanda's social and economic infrastructure.

new technologies for cooking, farming, and waste disposal that will be less harmful to the environment.

The government has established several programs to encourage women to go to school and to enter the world of business. Some of the goals set for the early 21st century are to establish more literacy programs outside the schools, to end discrimination against school-age mothers, to improve education in preventing sexually transmitted diseases such as HIV/AIDS, and to provide more help for women living in poverty. Rwanda has welcomed help from international organizations, such as the American Peace Corps.

RWANDA'S GENOCIDE MEMORIALS

Throughout Rwanda memorials to honor those killed in the genocide have been built. Gisozi, in Kigali, for example, is the burial site of more than 250,000 people killed during that three-month period. Photographs of those killed in the genocide are on display *(below)*. The educational purpose is stated in a brochure from the memorial: "Now that a million people have been murdered, we need to learn how and why such tragedies happen, in order to prevent them in the future."

Some visitors to the memorials are shocked by the display of victims' skulls and bones. A main purpose of such displays is to make certain that no one in the future can claim that there was no genocide, as some have tried to argue about the European Holocaust, in which 6 million Jews, and roughly 5 million others were murdered by the Nazis in the 1930s and early 1940s. At the memorial in Ntarama the church and another building have been left just as they were after some 5,000 bodies were removed in 1994. The scraps of clothing and personal items on the floor are powerful reminders of that awful event.

RELIGION

FROM THE 19TH CENTURY ON, Christianity has had a strong influence on Rwandan life. By the 1920s more than half the people had become Roman Catholic. Protestant missionaries have also gained converts and, today, various evangelical churches have been very successful, especially the Seventh Day Adventists.

Traditional, or tribal, religions have never disappeared, and many Rwandans seem to combine tribal traditions with Christian practices and beliefs. This mixing makes it difficult to determine the exact number of followers of each religion or denomination. According to the Rwandan Embassy in Washington, D.C., 56.5 percent of Rwandans are Roman Catholic, followed by 26 percent Protestant, 11 percent Adventist, and 4.6 percent Muslim. Only 0.1 percent are listed as followers of the traditional belief system.

Most outside observers say that at least one-quarter of the population continues to adhere to the traditional religion, even though they also worship at a Christian church or an Islamic mosque. Some social scientists also say that the followers of Islam (i.e., Muslims) make up close to 10 percent of the population rather than the government's figure of 4.6 percent.

Above: **A Muslim girl in Cyangugu. Islam was probably introduced to the country by Arab traders.**

Opposite: **A missionary church.**

TRADITIONAL BELIEFS

The traditional religion of Rwanda provides a number of clues that help explain why the people so readily accepted Christianity. Rwandans have always believed in a supreme being, for example, called Imana. This god

figure controls the entire world, but Rwanda is his home, and he returns there every night to rest. Many people continue to follow time-honored rituals involving Imana. The very name Imana is thought to have magical powers, so Rwandans often make use of it in naming children, as well as in sayings designed for such things as comfort, blessing, or promise. "Imana has blessed me with a son," would be a typical reference to this spiritual power, as would "May Imana make my cattle survive the disease."

Imana's name and power are also part of folktales and sayings. Many of these stories tell of people who received great gifts from Imana, then lost everything because they were greedy or disloyal.

These traditional beliefs also involve an element of fatalism, or the idea that events are part of a person's destiny. This idea of destiny begins early in a person's life. When a woman wants to become pregnant, for example, she places a few drops of water in a pitcher each night. This is in keeping with the notion that Imana is a potter who needs water to mix with the clay in the woman's womb.

When the child is born, Imana decides whether this person's life will be basically happy or troubled. Of course, people do not know right away what has been decided for this person. But in time, if the individual is stricken with illness, or falls into debt, or has a failed marriage, then people are likely to say that this person was created by Ruremakwaci. This is a name that describes Imana when, for whatever reason, he decides that a certain destiny will not be a happy one.

Another aspect of traditional religion that Rwandans can incorporate into their Christian beliefs is the idea of a life force, or soul, that remains in existence after a person dies. An animal's life force disappears at death, but in humans it turns into *bazimu*. These spirits of the dead reside in an underworld, Ikuzimu, and they keep the personality and even the name of the living person. Their existence is neither happy nor sad, but they do tend to linger around the places they once inhabited. The *bazimu* may live in the family home or in special huts made for them.

Most of the time, people are not pleased to feel that these spirits are present. They can bring illness, poor harvests, and poverty, most likely because they can no longer enjoy the pleasures of this life. Their power

A church in Kigali teems with worshipers. Though the population is predominantly Catholic, some experts estimate that up to a quarter of all Rwandans still practice their traditional religion.

THE CULT OF RYANGOMBE

An unusual cult that was part of the traditional Rwandan religion surrounded the mythical figure of Ryangombe. According to legend Ryangombe was a great warrior who was killed by a rampaging bull during a hunt. His distraught friends, not wanting to be separated from him, threw themselves onto the horns of the bull. Imana gave Ryangombe and his followers a special place: the Karisimbi volcano in the Virunga chain of seven volcanoes. The spirits of Ryangombe and his followers are said to live a happier existence than other *bazimu* do.

In the past this unusual cult seemed to be a unifying force in Rwandan society. A sort of brotherhood developed around the cult that included Hutu, Tutsi, and Twa members. Rituals and dances were held every July to honor Ryangombe, for which the members of the brotherhood painted their bodies and decorated special spirit huts. One member represented the spirit of Ryangombe and carried his spear. Even though the cult is disappearing in the early 21st century, it is remembered fondly for its idealistic encouragement of national unity and personal honor. A still-popular folk song recounts Ryangombe's exploits as a lover as well as a warrior.

over people is limited to members of their own clan, and troubled family members usually consult a diviner who may be able to send the spirit back to the underworld.

CHRISTIAN CHURCHES

Roman Catholic churches in Rwanda all seem to be large, like the enormous cathedral of Kabgayi, a few miles from Gitarama. It is the oldest in the country and completed in 1925. Even before the cathedral was built, missionaries were installed in Kabgayi in 1906, and it became the seat of Rwanda's first Catholic bishop.

Services are always well attended. Rwandans, with their love of music and dance, have always responded well to the colorful robes, the Gregorian chants, the processions, and the music. In the decades before independence there were also training schools there, where Rwandans could develop skills in areas such as carpentry, furniture making, printing, and blacksmithing. The Kabgayi Church Museum preserves the cultural history of the region as well as early religious artifacts.

Another famous cathedral, in Butare, is a large, red-brick structure built in the 1930s to honor Belgium's Princess Astrid. Visitors are often struck by the peacefulness of the enormous interior when the cathedral is

A service at Keboho Catholic Church.

empty. During services the sounds echo upward, adding to the beauty of the mass.

The role of the church during the civil war and genocide is ambiguous. Many church officials encouraged Hutu leaders in their drive for political power after independence, and some were swept along in the violence of the genocide. Many Tutsi and Hutu moderates flocked to the churches for protection in 1994. With their victims trapped inside, Hutu death squads tossed grenades through the windows, then finished off the slaughter with guns and machetes. Church officials were helpless to stop the slaughter, and some seem to have sided with the militia.

Many of these churches, like the hilltop church at Kibuye on Lake Kivu, remained damaged and empty for several years after the genocide. Finally, starting in about 2002, the churches were rebuilt. The Kibuye church now has new stained glass windows and new altar cloths. After standing some time as a memorial to the victims, the church is now open for religious services and a genocide memorial has been constructed next to it.

ISLAM IN RWANDA

In a bustling neighborhood of shops and stalls in southern Kigali, a muezzin's voice is heard issuing the Muslim call to public prayer. Nearby a large mosque, a Muslim house of worship, looms above the busy street. Muslims, as the followers of Islam are known, may make up as much as 10 percent of Rwanda's population, but this neighborhood in Kigali, known as Nyamirambo, is about the only place where their presence is visible. The religion was probably brought to Rwanda by Arab Muslim merchants in the 19th century.

Islam was founded in the seventh century by the Arab prophet Muhammad. Islam shares some beliefs with both Christianity and Judaism, including the belief in one God. Muslims also accept such Hebrew prophets as Abraham and Moses, and they regard Jesus as another great prophet, while Muhammad is considered the last and most important prophet.

Muslims are required to practice the Five Pillars of Islam: to recite the profession of faith at least once; to respond to the five daily calls to

VISIONS OF THE VIRGIN MARY

In 1981 a teenage girl named Alphonsine Mumereke and some friends saw visions of the Virgin Mary at the village of Kibeho. The visions continued, and the village drew pilgrims, first from Rwanda, then from other countries.

The village suffered terribly during the genocide, and its church was burned while sheltering survivors. Sightings of the Virgin have since resumed. Many visitors have been struck by the fact that such sightings have occurred on the eve of great warfare and destruction. For example, the visions of the Virgin at Medjugorje began in Yugoslavia just before that country exploded in civil war in the mid-1980s.

public prayer; to pay a special tax to support the poor; to fast every day during the holy month of Ramadan; and to perform, if they are able, the hajj, or pilgrimage, to the holy city of Mecca in Saudi Arabia.

A mosque, with its characteristic minarets, in the Nyamirambo district of Kigali.

LANGUAGE

RWANDA IS SOMETHING of a linguistic patchwork quilt, having four widely used languages. Kinyarwanda is the traditional language of the country and is spoken by everyone. French and English are also official languages. In addition, Swahili is a language commonly used in business and trade, not only in Rwanda but in all neighboring countries as well.

In spite of this mixing, language has been a unifying force rather than a divisive one. Since all groups use Kinyarwanda, the conflicts of the 1990s that led to civil war and mass murder were based on physical differences (real and perceived) that had nothing to do with languages.

LANGUAGE VARIATIONS

While everyone in Rwanda speaks Kinyarwanda and one other language, the second language varies. Most educated Rwandans who grew up in the country speak French. During the colonial period French was used by the Belgians, and Belgian Catholic officials taught it in their schools. Other educated Rwandans who grew up in exile, usually in Tanzania, Kenya, or Uganda, usually learned English as their second language. Those who rely on French as a second language may know very little English, and those who rely on English, in turn, often have little knowledge of French.

The government has not simplified matters by deciding that Rwandans should be trilingual—fluent in three languages. The three languages are Kinyarwanda, French, and English. Swahili will remain an unofficial language, not taught in the schools but acceptable for all those who want to use it in business. Because only about 70 percent of the people are literate, the challenge of becoming a trilingual nation seems enormous.

Above: **An advertisement in French invites passersby into a small hairdressing salon in Kigali. French is one of the three official languages of Rwanda.**

Opposite: **A rural boy takes a break from his chores to read.**

99

NONVERBAL COMMUNICATION

People in every culture communicate in many ways other than with words, including facial expressions, gestures, and body language. How people deal with time is also a behavior that sends messages. American businesspeople and representatives of aid agencies are frequently frustrated by the slow pace of business in Rwanda. Some come away with the feeling that a Rwandan official or businessperson is either incompetent or is trying to hide something. The truth, instead, is that business and government affairs in Rwanda are conducted at a much more relaxed pace.

Another way the treatment of time sends mixed messages is in holding meetings. Rwandans want business and government meetings to have a pleasant aspect. At the start of a meeting, for example, they prefer to spend some time exchanging pleasantries before talking business. They consider it rude to go right to the main topic. However, Americans and Europeans often show impatience with the slow pace. Rwandans interpret their facial expressions and behavior as signs that Westerners are pushy and aggressive.

Simple matters such as gestures also communicate and can require interpretation. Rwandans receive gifts with both hands or with the right hand only, while touching the right elbow with the left hand. Both of these gestures are expressions of gratitude. No words of thanks are necessary. A Westerner who gives a gift and does not hear a thank you may be offended or disappointed.

MEDIA

After the years of internal strife Rwanda is now starting to embrace instant communication. Cell phones are increasingly visible on the streets of Kigali and Butare, although not yet in rural areas. The use of personal computers, the Internet, and e-mail is developing more slowly, with only 25,000 Internet subscribers at the end of 2003.

In the mass media there are a number of radio stations, and these broadcast in Kinyarwanda, French, English, and Swahili. Rwandan television produces some local programming, primarily news. Most television, however, is relayed from other countries, including news broadcasts from England and the United States.

BANTU LANGUAGES

Bantu languages are a group within what is called the Niger-Congo language family. There are about 200 separate Bantu languages spoken by an estimated 60 million people occupying the southern third of the African continent. Both Kinyarwanda and Swahili are Bantu languages.

KIGALI PUBLIC LIBRARY

In 1999 the Kigali-Virunga Rotary Club voted to build a library *(above, under construction)* to start making up for the lack of books in Rwanda. Funds have been raised in Rwanda and from overseas donors, such as an organization called the American Friends of the Kigali Public Library (AFKPL) which has sent about $50,000. Although still short of funds, the Rotary Club hopes to have the library open in 2007. Supporters feel that the library can open a whole new world to young Rwandans and that literature can help develop a commitment to democracy and the peaceful resolution of ethnic conflicts.

Few Rwandans are readers, and this includes newspaper reading. There are several newspapers published in English. *The New Times* is published three times per week, with plans to publish daily, and *Rwanda Newsline* is published once a week.

PRONUNCIATION

Words in Kinyarwanda and Swahili are spelled phonetically, so every letter is pronounced. If a letter is written twice, it is pronounced twice—that is, it becomes two syllables. For instance, *mzee*, meaning "respected elder," is pronounced m-ZEE-ee. And in both languages the stress is usually on the second-to-last syllable.

SAMPLE WORDS AND PHRASES

English	French	Kinyarwanda	Swahili
Hello	*bonjour*	*muraho*	*salama*
Good-bye	*au revoir*	*muramukeho*	*kwa heri*
How are you?	*ça va?*	*amakura?/bitese*	*Hujambo?*
I'm fine.	*ça va bien*	*amakuru/meza*	*sijambo*
Please	*s'il vous plait*	*mubishoboye*	*tafadhali*
Thank you	*merci*	*murakoze*	*asante*
What's your name?	*Quel est votre nom?*	*witwande?*	*Jina lakonani?*
now	*maintenant*	*ubu/nonaha*	*sasa*
soon	*bientôt*	*vuba*	*sasa hivi*
today	*aujord'hui*	*none*	*leo*
yesterday	*hier*	*ejo hashize*	*jana*
tomorrow	*demain*	*ejo hazaza*	*kesho*

ARTS

RWANDA'S CULTURE is rich and varied. This artistic tapestry includes music, dance, folktales, poetry, painting, and a wide variety of handicrafts. Artistic expression is part of daily life. On any given day a visitor to a rural village might hear the pulsating rhythm of a half dozen *tambourinaires* (drummers), or watch a Twa master potter fashion a miniature water buffalo, or listen to fieldworkers repeat an ancient chant as they work.

For a number of years, especially during the chaotic early 1990s, the arts were neglected. But the arts have experienced a lively revival since 1995. Observers notice a renewed vigor in the songs and dances and an increased demand for Rwandan crafts from other countries. The government is helping by encouraging activities that involve art, crafts, and folklore.

RWANDA'S LITERARY TRADITION

Until the Europeans arrived in the 19th century, there was no written language used in Rwanda. Instead, all three ethnic groups developed a strong oral tradition made up of poems, songs, proverbs, and chants. These oral forms are still cherished today, long after the introduction of writing in Kinyarwanda, French, and English. Storytelling and the reciting of poetry continue to be popular, and skill in any form of public speaking is admired.

In Rwanda's preliterate society oral tradition provided a form of entertainment as well as a means of transmitting such information as history and moral lessons from generation to generation. The court of the *mwami* became a training place for young nobles to learn various literary forms, especially poems and songs that dealt with courage in battle. The Tutsi favored folklore dealing with the magnificence of their cattle, while the Twa composed poems and songs about their hunting skills. One of modern Rwanda's greatest writers, Alexis Kagame (1912–81), collected oral poetry and recorded many poems in Kinyarwanda and in French.

Opposite: **Traditional Tutsi musicians.**

MUSIC AND DANCE

The cultural life of Rwanda is based in tradition, with each artistic form dating back several hundred years. Music and dance are probably the most important of these forms, and both are woven into the fabric of people's daily lives. In addition to highly polished professional presentations, singing and dancing are built into ceremonies involving birth, marriage, death, the harvest, and hunting.

On the professional level the tall, splendidly attired Tutsi *intore* dancers, all male, are world renowned, and the *intore* dance troupe has toured in many countries. The *intore*, meaning "the chosen ones," were formed several centuries ago to perform exclusively at the royal court. Today performances are arranged by the National Museum in Butare.

The *intore* dances have changed in modern times. In the past *intore* performances were usually built around warlike themes. The dances had names like *umeheto* (the bow), *ingabo* (shield), and *ikuma* (the lance), and the men carried real weapons. Over the past century the weapons have

THREE MODERN AUTHORS

Very little modern literature has been written in Kinyarwanda. The most famous Rwandan authors have written in French.

Alexis Kagame was a man of broad intellectual achievements. Trained for the clergy, he was also a philosopher, ethnologist, and historian. He wrote about Rwanda's oral history and edited several volumes of the country's poetry, mythology, and folktales.

J. Saverio Naigiziki gained fame for his autobiography *Escapade rwandaise* (*Rwandan Adventure*) and also wrote a critically acclaimed novel, *L'Optimiste* (*The Optimist*), which deals with the marriage of a Hutu man and a Tutsi woman.

The best-known female writer is Yolande Mukagasana. She survived the genocide and moved to Europe, where she wrote two books, *La mort ne veut pas de moi* (*Death Doesn't Want Me*) and *N'aie pas peur de savoir* (*Don't Be Afraid to Know*), describing her experiences.

been replaced with replicas, and the dances now emphasize movement and rhythm rather than warfare.

The *intore* dancers were traditionally divided into two groups. One group, called the Indashyikirwa ("the unsurpassables") were all Tutsi. The second group, the Iishyaka ("those who challenge through their effort") were Twa dancers led by Tutsi.

The drama and power of the dance is heightened by the drum ensemble, usually containing seven to nine drums, which provides a strong, almost hypnotic set of complex rhythms. Melodic interludes are provided by the *lulunga*, a harplike instrument with eight strings.

The costumes consist of either a short skirt or a leopard skin wrapped around the legs. Crossed straps decorated with beads are worn across the chest, and a fringe of white colobus monkey fur is worn on the head. The total effect of the tall dancers, the movement, the music, and the costumes is one of power combined with grace.

Rwandans also create several forms of more modern music. In churches throughout the country, for example, devotional singing, with strong harmonies and an upbeat tone, can be heard.

Before the upheaval of the 1990s there were a number of bands and singers creating popular music, ranging from folk tunes to rock. During the 1990s many performers fled to Europe, especially Paris and Brussels (in Belgium). Bands with names like Imena, Les Fellows, Impala, and

A traditional Tutsi drum ensemble consisting of a full set of nine drums.

Abamarungu combined music from different parts of Africa, especially the Democratic Republic of the Congo, with Caribbean reggae and American rock. The music is colorful and lively and is now experiencing a comeback in Rwanda. New stars are also emerging, including Aimé Murefu, a guitarist who borrows from American guitarists, such as Jimi Hendrix and B. B. King.

CRAFTS

The people of Rwanda produce an amazing variety of crafts that display the artisans' great skill, including weavings, ceramics, paintings, jewelry, wood carvings, ironwork, and gourd containers. Over the centuries each craft has become highly specialized, and artisans pass on their skills, usually to a son or daughter. It would be difficult for an amateur weaver or potter to practice a craft without considerable training by a skilled artisan.

WEAVING

Weaving is done almost exclusively by women. They use several different fibers, including grasses, papyrus, and banana leaves, for weaving baskets and mats. Striking geometric patterns are woven in red, black, and white. Having a collection of baskets is regarded as a sign of status.

Women also weave smaller household items, such as pot holders and table mats, usually using banana leaves. They also weave small coils that are placed on a woman's head to help support large jugs and other objects. The weavings, which include hammocks and wall hangings as well as baskets of many sizes and designs, are sold at roadside stands and in the shops of craft cooperatives, such as ASAR (Association des Artistes Rwandais) in Kigali.

An unusual approach to weaving is seen in the Kuba cloth made in villages near Rwanda's border with the Democratic Republic of the Congo. Men make the basic cloth, weaving the central fibers of the palm leaf, and women then add an embroidered motif, creating a velvetlike fabric with an attractive geometric design. Long, horizontal shapes are intended to be wrapped around the hips and worn as a skirt. In the past small pieces of Kuba cloth were used as currency, but that practice died out around 1900.

WOOD CARVING

Most wood carving is done by men. In many families the wife is a weaver and the husband is a wood carver or sculptor. They make a variety of products, including bowls and jugs, tobacco pipes, stools, knife handles, and figurines. Men also make drums and other musical instruments.

A wood carver fashions an ornate figurine at the Kiaka Artisans Cooperative in Gisenyi.

POTTERY

Centuries ago the Twa were hunters and gatherers living in the mountainside forests of Central Africa. As more and more people moved into the regions and the forests were cleared for agriculture and pastureland, the Twa moved into the valleys. There they taught themselves to be outstanding potters without having access to special tools or the knowledge of kilns for firing their ceramics. They also developed great skill as dancers and became favored entertainers at the royal court. They sang and danced for the *mwami* and his family and made their pottery.

Twa potters gather clay from marshes in low valleys. They stomp the clay with their feet to soften it, then shape it with their hands. Their pottery is plain but sturdy and attractive. They make a variety of objects, including vases, flowerpots and cooking pots, stoves, candleholders, and all sorts of small figures of Rwanda's animals. The Twa fire their ceramics in a hole in the ground, covering the objects with a hot fire of grasses and twigs, topped with a layer of earth.

MODERN MARKETING

Until recently the lack of sales outlets had severely limited the earnings of artisans. Many men and women tried to sell their wares at roadside stands, where the items were often damaged by rain or road dust. Apart from market stalls in Kigali and other towns, there was no way to reach a larger public, especially tourists.

Since 2000 government agencies and international organizations have worked to expand the crafts market. Several government offices have displays of not only pottery, weavings, and carvings, but also of paintings, jewelry, and ironwork. Sales stalls have been established at airports, travel offices, and in some hotels. Rwanda's embassies and consulates are also promoting the country's crafts.

THE MOST UNUSUAL ART

In the town of Nyakarimbi, near the border with Tanzania, a group of artisans carries on a tradition of decorating houses with cow-dung paintings. These paintings, usually used to decorate interior walls, do indeed make use of cow dung. The surface is then painted in red and white, using colors made from clay, the sap of the aloe plant, and burned banana skins.

A women's group called the Kakira Association, formed in 1995, has revived the tradition and expanded it. Using the same natural materials, they produce colored tiles and panels, calling their products Iigongo art. The art is quite beautiful and has intricate geometric patterns. Sales have increased steadily every year.

LEISURE

EXCEPT FOR THE CHAOTIC YEARS of the 1990s, tourists have found Rwanda to be an attractive and unusual destination. It is a small, easily traveled country with beautiful scenery, and it offers an appealing variety of wildlife. The primates, and especially the unique mountain gorilla, draw visitors who hunt with cameras and binoculars rather than with guns. Rwandans are beginning to recognize the opportunities their country offers for tourists to enjoy the beauty and wonders of nature. Many young people in training to become workers and guides in the national parks and forests have discovered the fun and excitement of wildlife safaris and trekking for mountain gorillas or other primates.

Leisure activities have been severely limited by the fact that nearly 90 percent of the people live by farming or herding, and most of them are so poor that they have little time or money for leisure pursuits. Few Rwandans can spend an evening watching television, and other entertainment devices, such as VCRs, DVD players, and video games, are almost nonexistent. Nor do the vast majority of people have the opportunity to engage in organized activities, such as team sports, clubs, or activities, which require expensive equipment.

In spite of the limitations Rwandans do have fun. Even the poorest enjoy a variety of activities, including parties, family events, and a growing number of spectator sports. Television is available to only a few, but many people have radios, giving them an important connection with the rest of the world. The music that blares from storefronts, cafes, and pickup trucks would be familiar to most Americans.

Above: **A variety of western sports, including rugby, are played in Rwanda.**

Opposite: **A group of children play games using pebbles. Children in Rwanda do not have the resources to buy sophisticated toys. Instead they make do with whatever they can find and improvise games that are equally as fun as board games and electronic toys.**

RURAL ACTIVITIES

The majority of Rwandans work hard from first light to dark, herding sheep or goats, tending to crops, or creating crafts to sell. Children, too, work hard, carrying the day's supply of water or collecting enough firewood for cooking and heat. After the evening meal people do not have much time or energy for leisure pursuits.

Only the educated people of Rwanda are likely to be readers, and access to television is limited to people living in the few urban centers. But the country's oral tradition provides even the poorest families with an extensive "library" of poems, songs, riddles, folktales, proverbs, jokes, and games. Evenings spent around the glowing embers of a fire or the light of a kerosene lamp are likely to involve an elder telling stories or reciting poems, or an entire family singing.

Family gatherings provide more extended periods for enjoyment. Birthdays, weddings, naming parties, and holidays are filled with eating, playing games, and solving riddles or puzzles. Most noticeable at these occasions is the Rwandans love of music and dance. People of all ages can spend hours in fast-paced dances, often with the accompaniment of a single drum.

Rwandan children of all ages love playing games. Many are simple outdoor games, variations on such familiar contests as tag or hide-and-seek. Indoor games are equally popular, especially board games. The "board" is usually handmade, and the game pieces are seeds or pebbles. Some board-type games are even simpler, like one that involves tossing a half-dozen seeds into the air and catching as many as possible on the back of one's hand. Some board games, such as *mancala* and *igisoro*, have become popular in other countries and are now commercially published.

ENTERTAINMENT

Educated families in Rwanda, especially those with incomes well above the poverty line, have greater possibilities for leisure activities. While Rwanda has very few wealthy people, it does have a growing middle class. People who work in such fields as health care, government, business, banking, and education engage in activities more like those of Americans or Europeans.

Television is gradually becoming available, for example, at least in such urban centers as Kigali and Butare, although Rwanda has fewer TV sets per capita than any other country in Africa. And, as of 2005, the country also ranks low in per capita personal computers, and only 25,000 people are Internet subscribers. These numbers are increasing, but slowly.

Movies are also offering new entertainment possibilities. A movie theater was opened in the Kigali Business Center in 2001. It shows international films, one in the afternoon and another in the evening. Most of the films are in English, with subtitles in French. The addition of children's programs and the Planet Cinema Restaurant has turned the Business Center into an evening and weekend destination for family entertainment.

Even Kigali, by far the largest city, offers few additional entertainment facilities. The French-Rwandan cultural exchange arranges films, plays, and performances in music and dance. The tourist board also promotes Twa dance performances and visits to their pottery studios. The lively and colorful dances, sometimes humorous and often dramatic, last more

A tourist watches on as a young Rwandan girl climbs out of a hotel swimming pool in Gisenyi. Compared to their rural counterparts, urban Rwandans have better access to leisure facilities.

115

than two hours and are now becoming popular with Rwandan audiences, especially children.

Shopping is a favorite form of entertainment, especially on market days (usually Friday and Sundays). Several streets in Kigali and Butare are lined with shops and sandwich places, some selling local crafts, others a variety of European, African, and Indian wares. The markets are even more popular, drawing large, colorful, and noisy crowds. Open-air stalls are piled high with fresh foods, clothing, furniture, and housewares.

A growing number of middle-class Rwandans enjoy their evenings at restaurants, bars, and discos, where they mix with Europeans and Americans working with businesses or international agencies. Some establishments rely on DJs, but many have live bands playing African, European, and American music. Many Rwandans prefer eating at one of the quiet courtyard restaurants, tucked away from the bustling shopping areas. These moderately priced restaurants serve a variety of cuisines, including Chinese, Ethiopian, Indian, and Italian.

SPORTS

On a Saturday or Sunday afternoon cars, minibuses, and pedestrians fill the roads leading to Kisimenti crossroads on the outskirts of Kigali. Their destination is the Amahoro Stadium, where all major soccer (called football in Rwanda and the rest of the world) matches are played. The Amahoro experience is not much like a sports event in the United States. There is no scoreboard and no program listing the players. Children sell tickets outside, and the match starts more or less on time. But the game itself unfolds like soccer games everywhere, packed with suspense and excitement.

Perhaps the most surprising thing about Rwandan soccer is how well the national team plays and how good many of the local club teams have become. In October 2003, only nine years after the genocide, the national team qualified for the 2004 African Nations Cup. The team, known as Amavubi, or "Wasps," stung two more experienced teams—the Uganda Cranes and the Ghana Black Stars—to qualify. Although Rwanda did not win the cup, simply qualifying in a competition involving 52 African nations was a great morale booster for the country and has created a great surge of enthusiasm for soccer as well as other sports.

Since the late 1990s more and more secondary schools have developed soccer programs, and local communities have organized club teams. Other sports are also becoming popular. The Cercle Sportif, for example, located in Lower Kiyovu, has facilities for tennis, volleyball, basketball, swimming, and even badminton. Cycling, including mountain biking, is

A member of the national soccer team of Rwanda *(left)* tackles an opponent for the control of the ball in a World Cup qualifying match in 2006.

A TOUCH OF ANCIENT SUPERSTITION

When the Rwandan national team beat Uganda in 2003 in soccer, the Ugandans could not believe that their smaller, war-ravaged neighbor could win. They cried foul (or fowl!), claiming that the Rwandans had won through witchcraft by putting the remains of a chicken in the Ugandan goalmouth so that the Ugandan team could not score. Rwanda won 1 to 0.

gaining popularity, and even golf is now available at the Nyarutarama Golf Club.

Although none of these trends, except for the enthusiasm for soccer, is anything like a mass movement, the new interests are signs of Rwanda's progress. Each year more families find they have the free time and extra income to enjoy leisure activities. In addition, television, the Internet, and schools are making young people more aware of the possibilities, ranging from basketball to in-line skating.

A young Rwandan soccer fan cheers for his national team at an African Nations Cup match.

CRICKET IN RWANDA

One of the most unusual sports played in Rwanda is cricket. Most countries that play the unusual game have had a long association with Great Britain, such as India, Kenya, or Tanzania, which were all once British colonies. Rwanda did not have such an experience, but cricket is thriving.

The Rwanda Cricket Association lists several teams in Kigali and Butare, including some that represent foreign nationals living in Rwanda, including the British Community Team and three teams from the Asian community. Matches are played throughout the year, even in the rainy seasons, at the Kicukiro Secondary School in Kigali.

In June 2003 a well-attended match was held at the school, with England's Queen's XI playing the Rwanda Cricket Club. Several corporate sponsors, including Federal Express, had banners around the grounds. Rwanda hopes to introduce cricket in schools as a sport for boys and girls.

FESTIVALS

THE CELEBRATING OF FESTIVALS and holidays was largely suspended during most of the 1990s, but both secular and religious celebrations are back in full swing in the early 21st century. The combination of national holidays and religious events leads to a variety of celebrations. In addition, religious festivals are celebrated by Protestant, Roman Catholic, and Muslim Rwandans, and many of these contain variations derived from traditional tribal practices.

Some holidays have both secular and religious qualities. For example, New Year's Eve and New Year's Day are times for parties, dances, and lots of food. Roman Catholics also celebrate mass, and several Protestant churches also have services. Peace and National Unity Day on July 4 is a time to celebrate the end of the mass killings in 1994. It is also a time for solemn remembrance of the nearly 1 million people who perished.

A number of religious holidays follow a lunar calendar, which is based on the phases of the moon. Nearly all Muslim holidays are scheduled according to the lunar calendar. Every year a holiday falls about eleven days earlier than it did the year before. Some Christian holidays, such as Easter, are also scheduled according to the lunar calendar.

PUBLIC HOLIDAYS

The important national holidays are connected with independence and the restoration of peace in Rwanda after the genocide. National Day, July 1, celebrates achieving independence from Belgium in 1962 and the creation of the republic. Traditionally this is a day for parades, a review of the army, and speeches delivered by the president and other dignitaries, including representatives of Belgium's government.

Armed Services Day on October 26 has been a similar occasion. The government has felt it important to continue to display the power of

Opposite: **A jubilant** *intore* **dancer performs to the beat of traditional drums. Like music, dancing is inseparable from festivities in Rwanda.**

President Paul Kagame inspects Rwandan troops at an event held to mark Liberation Day on July 4.

Rwanda's military, not only out of pride for how swiftly the RPF's army ended the genocide, but also as a warning to Hutu rebels living in the Democratic Republic of the Congo or Burundi that Rwanda can handle any insurgency. Rwanda, however, has benefited from large sums of foreign aid, and some of the country's major financial supporters have expressed concern at the amount of resources devoted to military spending. In response the government has quietly scaled back the festivities.

The most important celebration is July 4—Peace and National Unity Day, also known as Liberation Day. This marks the success of the 1994 invasion by the RPF, which stormed into Rwanda, liberating terrified Tutsi and Hutu moderates who were hiding from the death squads. The celebration has always been one of huge relief and thanksgiving rather than one of exuberance.

Important events, such as Rwanda's 2003 1 to 0 soccer victory over Ghana, can lead to joyous, spontaneous celebrations. That celebration was an all-night affair, and the streets of Kigali were filled with people shouting and singing, accompanied by the noise of honking car and bus horns. The celebration was held in the same week as Independence Day and Liberation Day.

CHRISTIAN HOLIDAYS

There is a good deal of variety in the way different Christian churches celebrate holidays. This is true of Roman Catholic churches as well as Protestant, because some Catholic churches have rather loose ties with the official church. One reason for the variation is that many churches incorporate traditional tribal practices into their celebrations. At some holiday festivals it is not unusual to have tribal drums or *intore* dancers as part of a celebration of Christmas or All Saints' Day.

While nearly all churches, Catholic as well as Protestant, include at least some traditional tribal beliefs or practices, the extent varies from church to church. Some observers say that in many Protestant churches the festivals and services are more tribal than standard Protestant. In fact, some authorities say that as many as one-third of Rwandans should be classified as followers of indigenous (traditional) religions, while the official figure is 1 percent. When a Christian church celebrates All Saints' Day (November 1), for example, many in the congregation are likely to think of the Christian saints as *bazimu*, the spirits of the dead who reside in Ikuzimu (the underworld). Similarly, the Feast of the Ascension in May, the 40th day after Easter, which is celebrated by both Protestants and Catholics and marks the ascension of Jesus into Heaven, may be seen by many as a journey by Imana, the supreme being.

How much of traditional practice and belief enters into a particular church can often depend on the particular minister or priest. Some are willing to let the congregants maintain many of their ancient practices in

Women perform a traditional dance in Butare. Many churches have incorporated indigenous cultural practices into their religious celebrations.

order to keep them as members of the church. This is particularly true of some evangelical churches. Often led by charismatic preachers, these churches have won thousands of converts in the past 20 years, often by holding festivals consisting almost entirely of tribal music, songs, and dances.

Ministers and priests are also frequently invited to participate in tribal festivals that have been held for many centuries. Springtime, for example, is a time of renewal and planting, and every village celebrates with prayers, music, dances, processions, and special foods. Catholic or Protestant leaders easily fit their prayers and sermons into the other activities. Much the same occurs in the late summer, when the harvest festival is held on August 1. A number of villages also celebrate the harvest at other times, depending on when local crops are ready.

THE ISLAMIC MONTH OF RAMADAN

Somewhere between 5 and 10 percent of Rwandans are Muslim, most of whom live in Kigali and nearby towns. The most important period for Muslims is the month of Ramadan, which falls in the ninth month of the lunar calendar. During this 30-day period the faithful observe a very strict fast each day from first light until dusk. After dark they break the fast with a big family meal.

Following Ramadan the first two or three days in the month of Shawwal are the time for a joyous festival called Eid al-Fitr, meaning the Feast of the Fast Breaking. Muslims gather with family and friends for feasts, prayers, and the exchanging of gifts.

Other important Muslim holy days include Eid al-Kebir, which commemorates the moment when Abraham, about to sacrifice his son Ishmael to show obedience to God, is told not to harm the boy. This event is also commemorated in Judaism and Christianity. For Muslims the holy day coincides with the end of the hajj, the pilgrimage to Mecca. Another important day is Eid al-Moulid, the birthday of the prophet Muhammad.

CHRISTIAN HOLIDAYS

New Year's Day	January 1
Easter, including Good Friday, Holy Saturday, and Easter Monday	March/April
Ascension Thursday	May
Feast of the Assumption	August 15
All Saints' Day	November 1
Christmas	December 25

FOOD

THE FOODS OF RWANDA are similar to those of other countries in East Africa, especially Tanzania and Kenya. People enjoy a wide variety of fresh foods, including bananas, coconuts, mangoes, oranges, and pineapples, as well as an assortment of vegetables. The most common staples served with meat or fish are rice, boiled potatoes, or chips (french fries).

The diet of rural Rwandans is quite simple. One of the most common dishes is a cornmeal mixture called *ugali*, which looks something like mashed potatoes. *Ugali* is eaten plain or used to make *uji*, a kind of thin porridge. The standard bread, called *chapati*, is a flatbread with a rather sweet taste. Rural people rarely eat meat, but when they do, the favorites are either goat kebabs or a meat stew served with *ugali* or boiled potatoes.

Travelers find that most restaurants in Africa serve great chips, or french fries, and several European food critics say that Rwandan chips are the best on the continent.

Left: **A street vendor on the streets of Kigali with a huge comb of bananas to sell. Bananas are an important part of the Rwandan diet.**

Opposite: **A young mother prepares a meal for her family.**

Fresh *mandazi* being fried. Similar to doughnuts, they are often eaten as a snack or dessert.

Rwandans grow both white potatoes and sweet potatoes. White potatoes are called Irish potatoes, although no one knows why.

CITY VARIATIONS

People in Kigali and the larger towns generally have a more varied diet than do rural Rwandans. Most urban dwellers eat meat more frequently, and they also have a variety of restaurants from which to choose. Professional people and business managers often eat at restaurants specializing in various international cuisines, such as Chinese, French, Italian, and Indian. Many urban Rwandans prefer lower-priced restaurants, many of which serve buffet or cafeteria style. Restaurant meals built around chicken, steak, or fish are popular, with side dishes of boiled potatoes, rice, or chips. The most common fish is tilapia, a freshwater fish. Foreign visitors are often struck by the huge portions served in restaurants and the low prices.

Urban Rwandans also encounter a variety of fast foods. Some restaurants serve American-style hamburgers and pizza. Roadside stalls offer roasted corn, sodas, bottled water, and *mandazi*, sweet doughnuts.

Both city and rural families shop at open-air markets rather than at grocery stores or supermarkets. Fresh fruits and vegetables are displayed in

128

open crates and baskets. Shoppers fill their shopping bags with their selections rather than picking up prepackaged goods. Meats are purchased from a butcher, with chicken, beef, and goat being the most popular.

MEALTIME

Breakfast is usually a simple meal. Country people often have *mandazi*, fruit, and hot tea. In urban areas city workers often choose French bread or croissants rather than *mandazi*. Rwandan tea, called *chai* in Swahili, is often made by boiling water, tea, milk, and sugar together, creating a thick, sweet, milky concoction.

The main meal is usually served at midday, but this is changing among urban Rwandans. One reason for the decreasing emphasis on the noon meal is a new government regulation shortening the lunch hour of government workers. In addition, Rwandans who dine out with foreign businesspeople or aid workers find that it is much more convenient to eat the main meal in the evening.

Whenever it is served, the largest meal of the day is likely to include a stew made with beans or meat. Side dishes, in addition to boiled potatoes or rice, might include sweet potatoes, yams, *ugali* or *matoke* (cooked banana or plantain), and *chapati*. Beverages include milk or fruit juice for children, while adults are likely to have wine, a local beer called Primus, bottled water, *chai*, or sometimes coffee. Some country people enjoy a beer made from bananas that have been buried in the ground for several days.

A woman prepares coffee for taste testing in the Maraba district of southern Rwanda. Despite being famed for their coffee, few Rwandans drink the beverage.

RICE AND YAMS

In rural areas Rwandan women often make meals or dishes out of whatever ingredients are at hand, particularly when food is scarce. This recipe combines two of the most common foods in the country.
Makes 4 servings

2 yams, washed
1 cup white rice
2 cups water
1 teaspoon salt
Dash of lemon juice
$\frac{1}{4}$ teaspoon chili powder

Make 2 or 3 holes through the skin of the yams with a fork. Bake at 350°F for about 50 minutes or until soft when poked with a fork. While the yams are baking, cook the rice: bring the water to a boil in a medium-size (2-quart) saucepan. Add the salt and rice. Simmer for 20 minutes or until the rice is fluffy. Peel the cooked yams (or cut them in half and scoop out the center). Cut the yams in slices and add to the rice. Add the lemon juice and stir. Transfer the rice and yams to a serving dish. Sprinkle the chili powder over the top. Serve warm.

SWAHILI FRUIT SHAKE

Fresh fruit, especially banana and coconut, is used in many Rwandan desserts and beverages. This tasty fruit shake is a good example.

Makes 2 servings

1 scoop vanilla ice cream
1 pint milk
1 banana
4 tablespoons shredded coconut
$^1/_2$ teaspoon vanilla extract

Place the ice cream, milk, coconut, and vanilla extract in a mixing bowl or large pitcher. (You can use a blender if you prefer.) Peel the banana, cut it into thin slices, and add it to the mixture. Use an egg beater to beat the mixture thoroughly. You can use a whisk to stir the drink into a foamy shake. Serve immediately.

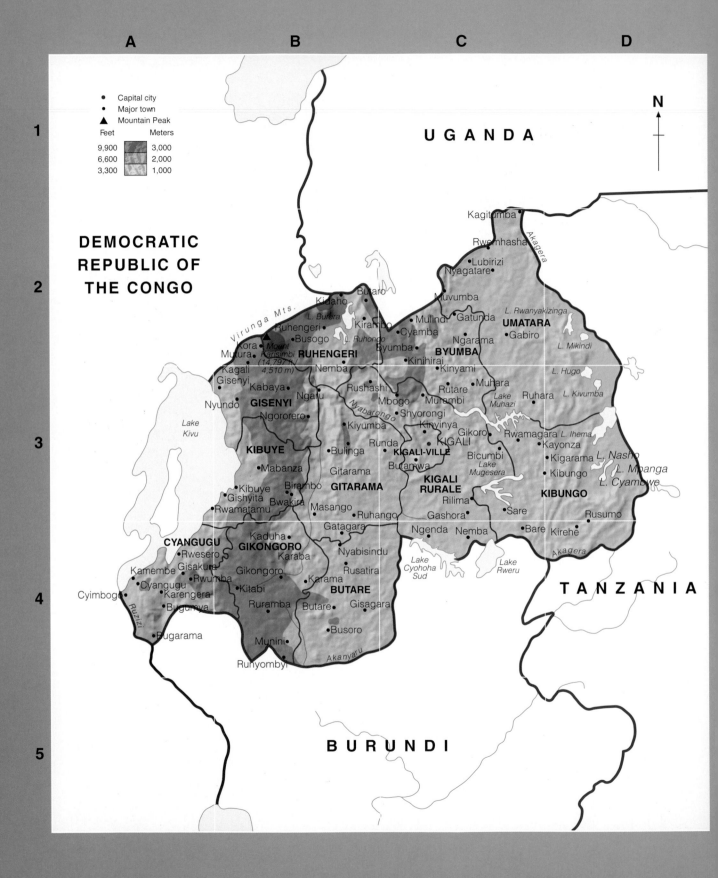

MAP OF RWANDA

Bicumbi, C3
Birambo, B3
Bugarama, A4
Bugumya, A4
Bulinga, B3
Busogo, B2
Busoro, B4
Butamwa, C3
Butare, B4
Bwakira, B3
Byumba, C2

Cyamba, C2
Cyangugu, A4
Cyimbogo, A4

Gabiro, C2
Gashora, C3
Gatagara, B4
Gatunda, C2
Gikongoro, B4
Gikoro, C3
Gisagara, B4
Gisakura, A4
Gisenyi, B3
Gishyita, B3
Gitarama, B3

Kabaya, B3
Kaduha, B4
Kagali, B2
Kagitumba, C2
Kamembe, A4

Karaba, B4
Karama, B4
Karengera, A4
Kayonza, C3
Kibungo, D3
Kibuye, B3
Kigali, C3
Kigarama, D3
Kinihirai, C2
Kinyami, C3
Kinyinya, C3
Kirambo, B2
Kitabi, B4
Kiyumba, B3
Kora, B2

Lake Burera, B2
Lake Cyambwe, D3
Lake Cyohoha Sud,
  C4
Lake Ihema, D3
Lake Kivu, A2–A4,
  B3
Lake Kivumba, D2
Lake Mikindi, D2
Lake Mpanga, D3
Lake Mugesera, C3
Lake Muhazi, C4
Lake Nasho, D3
Lake Ruhondo, B2
Lake Rwanyakizinga,
  D2
Lake Rweru, C4

Lubirizi, C2

Mabanza, B3
Masango, B3
Mbogo, C3
Mount Karisimbi,
  B2
Muhara, C3
Mulindi, C2
Munini, B4
Murambi, C3
Mutara, B2
Muvumba, C2

Nemba, B2
Nemba, C4
Ngarama, C2
Ngaru, B3
Ngenda, C4
Ngororero, B3
Nyabisindu, B4
Nyagatare, C2

Nyundo, B3

Rilima, C3
Ruhango, B3
Ruhara, C3
Ruhengeri, B2
Runda, C3
Runyombyi, B4
Ruramba, B4
Rusatira, B4
Rushashi, B3
Rutare, C3
Rwamagara, C3
Rwamagara, C3
Rwamatamu, A3
Rwemhasha, C2
Rwesero, A4
Rwumba, A4

Sare, C3
Shyorongi, C3

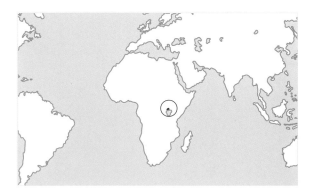

133

ECONOMIC RWANDA

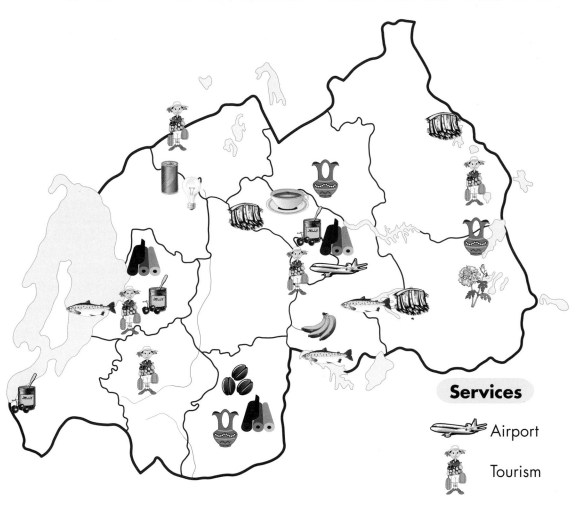

Services

 Airport

Tourism

Manufacturing

 Food Products

 Handicrafts

 Textiles

Agriculture

 Bananas

 Chrysanthemums

 Coffee

 Tea

Natural Resources

 Fish

 Hydroelectricity

 Tin Ore

Tungsten Ore

ABOUT THE ECONOMY

GROSS DOMESTIC PRODUCT (GDP)
$10.3 billion (2004 estimate)

PER CAPITA GDP
$1,300

GDP GROWTH RATE
5 percent (2004 estimate)

GDP SECTORS
Agriculture 41.1 percent, industry 21.2 percent, services 37.7 percent

LAND AREA
10,169 square miles (26,338 square km)

AGRICULTURAL PRODUCTS
Coffee, tea, bananas, pyrethrum

MINERALS
Gold, tungsten (wolframite), tin (cassiterite), methane, hydroelectric power

CURRENCY
Rwandan Franc (RWF)
USD 1 = 551.25 (June 2006)

INDUSTRIES
Agricultural products, shoes, soap, furniture, textiles, cement

MAJOR EXPORTS
Coffee, tea, pyrethrum, tin ore

EXPORT PARTNERS
Indonesia, China, Germany (2004)

MAJOR IMPORTS
Foodstuffs, machinery, steel, petroleum products, construction materials

IMPORT PARTNERS
Kenya, Germany, Belgium, Uganda, France

LEADING FOREIGN INVESTORS
Belgium, France, Germany, Great Britain

INFLATION RATE
7 percent (2004 estimate)

POVERTY RATE
60 percent (2002 estimate)

CULTURAL RWANDA

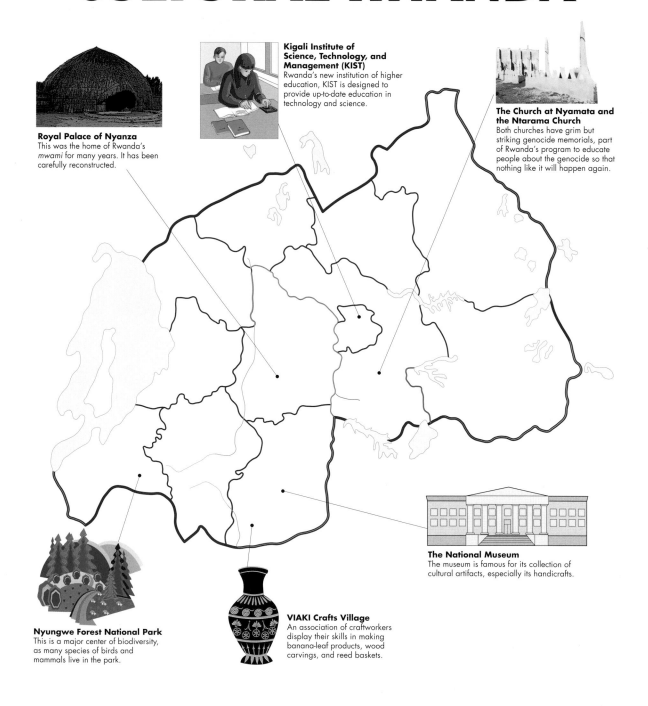

Royal Palace of Nyanza
This was the home of Rwanda's *mwami* for many years. It has been carefully reconstructed.

Kigali Institute of Science, Technology, and Management (KIST)
Rwanda's new institution of higher education, KIST is designed to provide up-to-date education in technology and science.

The Church at Nyamata and the Ntarama Church
Both churches have grim but striking genocide memorials, part of Rwanda's program to educate people about the genocide so that nothing like it will happen again.

The National Museum
The museum is famous for its collection of cultural artifacts, especially its handicrafts.

Nyungwe Forest National Park
This is a major center of biodiversity, as many species of birds and mammals live in the park.

VIAKI Crafts Village
An association of craftworkers display their skills in making banana-leaf products, wood carvings, and reed baskets.

ABOUT THE CULTURE

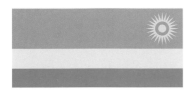

OFFICIAL NAME
Republic of Rwanda

NATIONAL FLAG
Three horizontal bands of sky blue, yellow, and green, plus a golden sun with 24 rays in the top right-hand corner. The flag has no red; the artist chose instead "the colors of peace."

NATIONAL ANTHEM
Rwanda Nziza, Beautiful Rwanda

CAPITAL
Kigali

OTHER MAJOR CITIES
Butare

POPULATION
8,440,820 (2005 estimate)

URBAN POPULATION
18.3 percent

POPULATION DENSITY
826 per square mile (319 per sq km)

ETHNIC GROUPS
Hutu 90 percent, Tutsi 9 percent, Twa 1 percent

RELIGIOUS GROUPS
Roman Catholic 57 percent, Protestant 26 percent, Muslim 5 percent

TIME
Greenwich Mean Time (GMT) plus 2 hours

LIFE EXPECTANCY
Male 45.92 years, Female 48.03 years

OFFICIAL LANGUAGES
Kinyarwanda, French, English

EDUCATION
Free and compulsory for ages 7 to 12.

LITERACY RATE
Male 76.3 percent, Female 64.7 percent (2003 estimate)

NATIONAL HOLIDAYS
New Year's Day (January 1), Democracy Day (January 28), Labor Day (May 1), National Day (July 1), Peace and Unity Day (July 5), Armed Forces Day (October 26)

FAMOUS RWANDANS
Paul Kagame—military leader who led the 1994 RPF invasion that ended the genocide; elected fifth president in April 2000; reelected 2003.

TIME LINE

IN RWANDA	IN THE WORLD
10,000 B.C. Earliest settlements in Rwanda are established. The Twa hunt and gather.	
	753 B.C. Rome is founded.
700 B.C. Hutus move in and force the Twa off their farmland.	
200 B.C. Tutsi gain dominance.	
	116–17 B.C. The Roman Empire reaches its greatest extent, under Emperor Trajan (98–17).
	A.D. 600 Height of Mayan civilization
	1000 The Chinese perfect gunpowder and begin to use it in warfare.
15th century Tutsi leader Ruganzu Bwimba establishes a kingdom near Kigali.	
	1530 Beginning of transatlantic slave trade organized by the Portuguese in Africa.
	1558–1603 Reign of Elizabeth I of England
	1620 Pilgrims sail the *Mayflower* to America.
	1776 U.S. Declaration of Independence
	1789–99 The French Revolution
19th century Kigeri Rwabugiri expands kingdom to its present borders.	**1861** The U.S. Civil War begins.
	1869 The Suez Canal is opened.
1885 The Berlin Conference. Germany claims Ruanda-Urundi as part of German East Africa.	
1890s Arrival of Europeans	
1911–12 German troops help the Tutsi incorporate Hutu regions into Rwanda.	

IN RWANDA	IN THE WORLD
1914–18 Belgium takes control of Rwanda.	**1914** World War I begins.
1923 League of Nations creates Ruanda-Urundi as a League Mandate to be ruled by Belgium.	**1939** World War II begins.
	1945 The United States drops atomic bombs on Hiroshima and Nagasaki.
	1949 The North Atlantic Treaty Organization (NATO) is formed.
1950s Belgians switch their support from the still-powerful Tutsi minority to the Hutu majority.	**1957** The Russians launch Sputnik.
1962 Rwanda becomes an independent republic. Grégoire Kayibanda is elected president	**1966–69** The Chinese Cultural Revolution
1973 Major General Juvénal Habyarimana overthrows Kayibanda in a military coup and seizes power.	**1986** Nuclear power disaster at Chernobyl in Ukraine
1990 Rwandan Patriotic Front (RPF) launches invasion.	**1991** Break-up of the Soviet Union
1993 The Arusha agreement is signed.	
1994 Habyarimana is killed in a plane crash. Hutu extremists launch a genocide against the Tutsis. Hundreds of thousands are massacred. The RPF invades, and on July 4, the RPF captures Kigali. On July 18 cease-fire is declared. Pasteur Bizimungu is elected president.	**1997** Hong Kong is returned to China.
2000 In March Bizimungu resigns; Paul Kagame, is sworn in as president.	**2001** Terrorists crash planes in New York, Washington, D.C., and Pennsylvania.
2003 Paul Kagame is reelected.	**2003** War in Iraq

GLOSSARY

abiiru
A powerful group of advisers in the early Rwandan kingdoms.

bazimu
Spirits of the dead in traditional Rwandan religion.

chai
Swahili word for sweetened hot tea.

chapati
A sweet-tasting flatbread.

gacaca
Community courts established to try thousands of Hutu accused of the 1994 genocide.

genocide
The deliberate destruction of an ethnic group.

hajj
The pilgrimage to Mecca by Muslims.

Ikuzímu
The underworld in traditional Rwandan religion.

Imana
The supreme being (God) in traditional Rwandan religion.

Interahamwe
Militia units created by the army in 1990; later known as death squads.

intore
Famous Rwandan dance troupes.

Kinyarwanda
The language of Rwanda.

mandazi
A sweet doughnut, often eaten for breakfast.

raptors
Birds of prey, such as eagles and hawks.

Ryangombe
A religious cult built around the legend of a great Rwandan warrior.

Swahili
A Bantu language widely used throughout East Africa.

tambourinaires
Drummers that accompany intore dancers.

ubuhake
The feudal social system in which the person of power provided protection for the weaker partner in exchange for services.

ugali
A thick cornmeal mixture, eaten as is or used to make a porridge called *uji*.

FURTHER INFORMATION

BOOKS

Fossey, Dian. *Gorillas in the Mist*. London: Orion Publishing Group, 2001.

Gourevitch, Philip. *We wish to inform you that tomorrow we will be killed with our families; Stories from Rwanda*. New York: Picador, 1999.

Keane, Fergal. *Season of Blood—A Rwandan Journey*. New York: Penguin, 1997.

Kingdon, Jonathan. *Island Africa*. Princeton, NJ: Princeton University Press, 1990.

Lewis, Jerome & Knight, Judy. *The Twa of Rwanda*. World Rainforest Movement, 1996.

Mowat, Farley. *Woman in the Mists*. New York: Warner Books, 1988.

WEB SITES

allAfrica.com. www.allafrica.com

Embassy of the Republic of Rwanda in Washington, D.C. www.rwandemb.org

USAID Rwanda www.rwanda1.com

VIDEOS

Gorillas in the Mist, 1988.

Hotel Rwanda, 2005.

BIBLIOGRAPHY

Barnett, Michael. *Eyewitness to a Genocide: The United Nations and Rwanda*. Ithaca, NY: Cornel University Press, 2003.

Booth, Janice and Philip Briggs. *Rwanda*. Chalfont St. Peter, England: Brandt Travel Guides, 2004.

Fegley, Randall, editor. *Rwanda—World Bibliographical Series, volume 154*. ABC-Clio, 1993.

Halsey Carr, Rosamond and Ann Howard Halsey. *Land of a Thousand Hills*. New York: Viking, 1999.

Stuart, Chris and Tilde Stuart. Africa's Vanishing Wildlife. Washington, D.C.: Smithsonian Books, 1996.

INDEX